TRANSPARENCY

WARREN BENNIS
DANIEL GOLEMAN
JAMES O'TOOLE
with PATRICIA WARD BIEDERMAN

TRANSPARENCY

How Leaders Create a Culture of Candor

JOSSEY-BASS
A Wiley Imprint
www.josseybass.com

Published by Jossey-Bass
A Wiley Imprint
989 Market Street, San Francisco, CA 94103-1741—www.josseybass.com

Jossey-Bass books and products are available through most bookstores. To contact Jossey-Bass directly call our Customer Care Department within the U.S. at 800-956-7739, outside the U.S. at 317-572-3986, or fax 317-572-4002.

Jossey-Bass also publishes its books in a variety of electronic formats. Some content that appears in print may not be available in electronic books.

Library of Congress Cataloging-in-Publication Data

Bennis, Warren G.
  Transparency : how leaders create a culture of candor / Warren Bennis, Daniel Goleman, James O'Toole ; with Patricia Ward Biederman.—1st ed.
    p. cm.
  Includes bibliographical references.
  ISBN 978-0-470-27876-5 (cloth)
  1. Disclosure of information. 2. Corporate governance. 3. Organizational culture. I. Goleman, Daniel. II. O'Toole, James. III. Title.
  HD2741.B386 2008
  658.4'038—dc22

                                                        2008007570

Printed in the United States of America
FIRST EDITION
HB Printing   10 9 8 7 6 5 4 3 2

CONTENTS

PREFACE   vii
Warren Bennis

1 CREATING A CULTURE OF CANDOR   1
Warren Bennis, Daniel Goleman, and Patricia Ward Biederman

2 SPEAKING TRUTH TO POWER   45
James O'Toole

3 THE NEW TRANSPARENCY   93
Warren Bennis

NOTES   123

THE AUTHORS   129

Warren Bennis

PREFACE

Certain issues leap to the fore across institutions and start to enter almost all our conversations about organizations, business, public life, and our personal realities. Transparency is one of those urgent, increasingly prominent issues.

As someone who has devoted much of his life to the study of leaders, I find myself talking about transparency—and thus about trust as well—whenever I talk about leadership. Transparency is a central issue whether the subject is global business, corporate governance, national and international politics, or how the media deal with the tidal wave of information that slams into us each day. An inclusive and appealing word, transparency encompasses candor, integrity, honesty, ethics, clarity, full disclosure, legal compliance, and a host of other things that allow us to deal fairly with each other. In a networked universe, where competition is global and reputations can be shattered by the click of a mouse, transparency is often a matter of survival. As stakeholders in many different organizations, we increasingly clamor for transparency, but what are we truly asking for? What is the promise of transparency? And what are its very real risks? How should leaders and organizations think about transparency—and why is it essential that leaders understand it? In this book, I join with fellow authors and veteran students of organizational life Dan Goleman, James O'Toole, and my longtime collaborator Patricia Ward Biederman to explore what it means to be a transparent leader, create a transparent organization, and live in an ever-more-transparent world culture. This book makes no claims to be the last word on this complex subject. But we believe these three interconnected essays offer insights that will help leaders think more clearly and act more thoughtfully in matters relating to transparency, an issue that becomes ever more important as this fascinating, difficult era unfolds.

Trust and transparency are always linked. Without transparency, people don't believe what their leaders say. In the United States, many of us have lived with the sense that the government has been keeping things from us, and many mistrust the explanation that our leaders must do so because the truth would empower our enemies. Many of us believe the lack of transparency is the real enemy.

Transparency is so urgent an issue in large part because of the emergence in the last decade of ubiquitous digital technology that makes transparency all but inevitable. We live in an era when communication has never been easier, nor more relentless. More and more of our experience is being stored electronically, and powerful search engines allow this swelling archive to be mined in a matter of seconds by anyone with Internet access.

This new technology is literally emancipating millions of people who once lived in isolation within the confines of their villages, and it offers all of us endless new possibilities. At the same time, the new technology has ramped up the ambient level of anxiety in daily life as we increasingly live roped to our personal digital assistants, cell phones, and other beeping, glowing devices.

Paradoxically, greater transparency has brought bewilderment as well as enlightenment, confusion as well as clarity. Each new revelation, much as we long for it, reminds us that the ground is not solid beneath our feet. We are uneasily aware that the present has no shelf life. Although we know more than ever, we often feel less in control. Our world seems simultaneously more anarchic and more Orwellian, more and less free.

These three essays look at transparency from three different vantage points—within and between organizations, in terms of personal responsibility, and finally in the context of the new digital reality—all with an emphasis on how these relate to leaders and leadership. In the first essay Dan Goleman, Pat Ward Biederman, and I explore an urgent dilemma for every contemporary leader: how to create a culture of candor. We argue that the unimpeded flow of information is essential to organizational health. Best known for his work on emotional intelligence, Dan has been doing research for decades on how information flow shapes organizations. He has a longstanding interest in self-deception and how it skews decision making. And he is fascinated by the role "vital lies" play in keeping essential truths from surfacing, first in families and later in businesses and other organizations. For my part, I have long considered candor essential for personal and organizational health; denying the truth harms us immeasurably. Organizations need candor the way the heart needs oxygen. Ironically, the more corporate and political leaders fight transparency, the less successful they are. The reason for this is not, unfortunately, the inevitable triumph of good over evil but the reality-shifting power of the new technology. Whether leaders like it or not, thanks to YouTube, there is no place to hide.

Jim O'Toole's essay has the provocative title "Speaking Truth to Power," a prerequisite for transparency and a responsibility we too often fail to fulfill. An author, consultant, and professor of business and ethics with a passion for philosophy as well as a degree in social anthropology, Jim brings an expansive frame of reference to bear on this critical topic. Citing Sophocles, Shakespeare, sociobiology, and General Shinseki, he includes a provocative analysis of Aristotle's belief that virtue requires becoming angry at the things that warrant anger. Jim also describes his unforgettable encounter with Donald Rumsfeld at an Aspen Institute seminar.

My final essay explores what I call "the new transparency." It shows how digital technology is making the entire world more transparent. Because of technology, leaders are losing their monopoly on power, and this has positive impacts—notably the democratization of power—as well as some negative ones.

In the following pages, we talk about whistleblowers and Second Life, groupthink, and blogging as an act of resistance. We show how digital technology is driving the new transparency, one that is paradoxically both more and less dependent on the will of the individual. But ultimately this is not a book about technology. It is about the things that have mattered since the new technology was the flint and the longbow—courage, integrity, candor, responsibility. Technologies change. Human nature doesn't. It is our hope that what you read here will help you embrace transparency, a good thing but rarely an easy one. Combining theory and experience, our book offers both a long view of transparency and practical advice. We hope you will find ideas in each essay to make you a better follower, a better leader.

Santa Monica, California   Warren Bennis
March 2008

TRANSPARENCY

1

Warren Bennis, Daniel Goleman,
and Patricia Ward Biederman

CREATING A CULTURE OF CANDOR

In the spring of 2007 something unprecedented happened in the southern Chinese city of Xiamen. In a nation notorious for keeping citizens in the dark, word got out that a petrochemical plant was to be built near the center of the lovely port city. The factory would have produced toxic paraxylene, and residents who learned of the plans were understandably alarmed. A decade ago, concerned Chinese citizens could have done little to stop the plant's construction. But this is a new age, not just in China but throughout the world. Via e-mail, blogs, and text messages, word of the plan spread and a protest was organized against it. As the *Wall Street Journal* reported, hundreds, perhaps thousands of protesters gathered at Xiamen's city hall to oppose the plant.[1] Chinese officials refused to acknowledge the protest and shut down Web sites that opposed the plant. But using today's ubiquitous communication technology protestors were able to circumvent the official silence. Participants took photos of the protest with their cell phones and posted them on the Web. Much to the chagrin of Chinese officials, some photos were transmitted straight to sympathetic media. The result was a victory of electronics-driven light over official darkness. City officials have postponed construction of the plant until a new study of its environmental impact is completed.

Today the word *transparency* pops up in stories about everything from corporate governance to the activities of the U.S. Justice Department. In the mouths of those in power, its meaning tends to be fuzzy, although, as *New York Times* essayist John Schwartz writes, when officials say they are being transparent, "what they really mean is 'not lying' and 'not hiding what we're really doing.' But that doesn't sound as nice or vague, does it?"[2] The vagueness is understandable, however. As we all know, claiming to be transparent is not the same as actually *being* transparent. Even as many heads of corporations and even of states boast about their commitment to transparency, the containment of truth continues to be a dearly held value of many organizations. Sadly, you can say you believe in transparency without practicing it or even aspiring to it.

While opacity is far less of a problem in the United States than in some other nations, it continues to characterize many, if not most, American organizations. And lack of transparency is usually no accident. It is often systematically built into the very structure of an organization. In the following pages, we look at the forces that conspire against an organizational culture of candor and transparency, and the often disastrous results when those qualities are lacking. We also show that the effort to withhold information from the public has become an all-but-impossible task because of profound changes in the global culture. Most important of these is the emergence of electronic technology that facilitates sunlight, and the rise, over the last decade, of the blogosphere—a development that has made transparency all but inevitable. In today's gotcha culture, no men's room tryst is sure to remain secret, no racial slur goes unrecorded, no corporate wrongdoing can be safely entombed forever in a company's locked file cabinets. A decade ago, secrets often remained buried until a professional journalist could be persuaded to reveal them. Today anyone with a cell phone and access to a computer has the power to bring down a billion-dollar corporation or even a government.

WHAT IS A CULTURE OF CANDOR?

When we speak of transparency and creating a culture of candor, we are really talking about the free flow of information within an organization and between the organization and its many stakeholders, including the public. For any institution, the flow of information is akin to a central nervous system: the organization's effectiveness depends on it. An organization's capacity to compete, solve problems, innovate, meet challenges, and achieve goals—its intelligence, if you will—varies to the degree that information flow remains healthy. That is particularly true when the information in question consists of crucial but hard-to-take facts, the information that leaders may bristle at hearing—and that subordinates too often, and understandably, play down, disguise, or ignore. For information to flow freely within an institution, followers must feel free to speak openly, and leaders must welcome such openness.

No matter the official line, true transparency is rare. Many organizations pay lip service to values of openness and candor, even writing their commitment into mission statements. Too often these are hollow, if not Orwellian, documents that fail to describe the organization's real mission and inspire frustration, even cynicism, in followers all too aware of a very different organizational reality.

When we talk about information flow, we are not talking about some mysterious process. It simply means that critical information gets to the right person at the right time and for the right reason. Although the successful flow of information is not automatic and often requires the leader's commitment, if not intervention, it happens every day in organizational life, often in the most mundane ways. For instance, a few years ago, General Electric became alarmed about a precipitous drop in appliance sales. At meetings on the matter, the conversation soon narrowed to how the problem could be solved by improving marketing: should GE focus on pricing? On advertising? On some other change in marketing strategies?

Then someone from the company's financial services arm, GE Capital, spoke up. He put up a PowerPoint presentation showing that consumer debt had reached near-saturation levels. The problem wasn't that GE was failing to market its appliances successfully. The likelier problem was that customers were too strapped to buy the big-ticket items that GE sold. That single crucial bit of information swiftly shifted the conversation from marketing to financing, as the company began seeking ways to help customers pay for appliances. The right information had found its way to the right people at the right time.

Just as the free flow of information can maximize the likelihood of success, damming its flow can have tragic consequences. An instructive example is the decision of Guidant executives to continue selling their Contak Renewal defibrillators even after they learned that the implanted heart regulators were prone to electrical failures implicated in the deaths of at least seven patients.

Because company officials remain silent on the matter, we can only speculate on why the firm decided not to recall the devices until 2005, three years after insiders learned of the flaw. Perhaps the health-sciences firm was blinded by its then-anticipated acquisition by Johnson & Johnson (it has since been acquired by Boston Scientific). Perhaps its corporate judgment was clouded by its Yale-Harvard-like competition with Medtronic, the leading manufacturer of implantable defibrillators. Whatever Guidant's reasoning, the result was not only needless deaths but a catastrophic trust problem with its primary customers—not heart patients but the physicians who prescribe the lucrative life-saving devices. According to the *New York Times,* Guidant's share of the defibrillator market dropped from 35 percent to about 24 percent after the recall, apparently because of the disgust many physicians felt at the company's decision to conceal an embarrassing truth on which patients' lives literally depended. As one angry physician wrote to the firm: "I am not critical of Guidant's device problems—these devices are so complex, issues are expected. I will not, however, work with a company that put profit and image in front of good patient care and honesty in device manufacturing."[3]

CHOOSING TRANSPARENCY

It almost goes without saying that complete transparency is not possible—nor is it even desirable, in many instances. Just as national security concerns may justify limiting access to certain information to a small number of carefully vetted individuals, an organization may have a legitimate interest in holding close and guarding from competitors information about innovations, original processes, secret recipes, or corporate strategies. Such secrets are reasonable. However, secretiveness is often simply reflexive. And secretive organizations are vulnerable to exposure by both the mainstream media and their growing legions of amateur competitors. But even when lack of candor is likely to be harmful, many organizations continue to choose it over openness, as Guidant appears to have done.

Because the term *transparency,* like *courage* and *patriotism,* has the exalted ring of eternal truth, it is easy to forget that transparency is a choice. Writer Graeme Wood gives a vivid illustration of this in his analysis in the *Atlantic* of how differently recent U.S. administrations have treated sensitive information.[4] Arguing that the administration of President George W. Bush is unprecedented in its insistence on secrecy, Wood says the current trend began in 1982 with Ronald Reagan, whose philosophy was, in effect, "When in doubt, classify." By 1985, 15 million documents had been classified, far more than had been shrouded under President Carter. President Bill Clinton, who favored declassification, ushered in a new era, saying, in effect, "When in doubt, let it out." Classification surged again under George W. Bush. In 2006, 20.6 million documents were classified, more than six times the 3.6 million classified under Clinton. "Leaving aside the blinkering effect it has on congressional oversight, too much secrecy impedes the routine functioning of the executive branch, by making useful information difficult for many government employees to see," Wood argues. Ironically, he points out, secrecy also has the unintended consequence of making leaks more likely.

Another dramatic example of transparency as choice was the 2007 decision by the Central Intelligence Agency director, General Michael V. Hayden, to declassify the agency's so-called family jewels. Buried by Director William E. Colby in 1973, these are internal documents relating to some of the agency's most controversial activities, including attempts to assassinate Cuban leader Fidel Castro. Hayden appears to have opted for sunlight because he believes revealing even ugly truths would ultimately help the agency. As the *New York Times* reported: "Hayden said it was essential for the C.I.A., an organization built on a bedrock of secrecy, to be as open as possible in order to build public trust and dispel myths surrounding its operations. The more that the agency can tell the public, he said, the less chance that misinformation among the public will 'fill the vacuum.'"[5]

But few leaders in either the public or private sector have been willing, as Hayden was, to choose voluntary transparency. Following Enron's meltdown and the other transparency-related scandals that did such damage to the American economy in recent years, long-needed reforms were enacted. Though flawed, and with unintended consequences of its own, the Sarbanes-Oxley Act has helped make corporate governance more transparent. But legislation alone cannot make organizations open and healthy. Only the character and will of those who run them and participate in them can do that. New regulations can help restore much-needed trust, but they can only go so far. If a culture of collusion exists instead of a culture of candor, participants will find ways around the rules, new or old, however stringent. Candor and transparency become widespread only when leaders make it clear that openness is valued and will be rewarded. Openness happens only when leaders insist on it.

The influence of a leader committed to transparency was evident in the 2007 decision by heads of the New York City Health and Hospitals Corporation to release information on mortality and infection rates at the eleven hospitals it operates.[6]

The largest public health system in the United States, the corporation decided to act in spite of opposition from a notoriously secretive hospital industry in hopes of reducing the rising number of preventable infections and subsequent deaths among the 1.3 million patients treated in its hospitals each year. The corporation was encouraged in its pioneering move by New York City Mayor Michael R. Bloomberg. A crusader for transparency, who believes it encourages collaboration and positive change, Mayor Bloomberg created a free 311 phone line so New Yorkers can directly report their concerns (more than 49 million so far). According to a 2007 profile in *Business Week*, the 311 line is an example of bottom-up transparency that allows Bloomberg to gauge New Yorkers' attitudes as well as their problems.[7] Bloomberg also eschews a private office to work among his aides in a "see-through city hall" with windows in the meeting rooms so the public can literally watch the city's business being conducted.

WHISTLEBLOWERS, THEN AND NOW

The most damaging secrets within organizations are often those that deal with activities that cause harm—exploding gas tanks, brittle O-rings, secret prisons where a jauntily named horror called water-boarding takes place. The exposure of such embarrassing, even shameful, secrets is transparency at its best and most difficult. Traditionally, such secrets have come to public attention because of whistleblowers, courageous individuals who expose their organizations' deepest secrets, often at considerable peril to themselves. (In Essay Two, James O'Toole continues the discussion of whistleblowers.) Sociologist Myron Glazer has studied several hundred whistleblowers in government and industry, and found that almost inevitably the person who exposes wrongdoing suffers, usually by being shunned, demoted, fired, or otherwise punished.

A classic example is Specialist Samuel J. Provance, who revealed that detainees at Iraq's Abu Ghraib prison were being abused by their American captors. A U.S. Army intelligence officer, Provance went public only after he was unable to galvanize his superiors to take action. As an apparent result of his candor, Provance was demoted, lost his security clearance, and was sent to Germany, where, he says, he is assigned to "picking up trash and guard duty."[8]

That kind of retaliation is what keeps most people from telling explosive secrets, whether in families or organizations. Although whistleblowers are often exiled from their organizations for their unwanted candor, Glazer's study revealed that they almost always found the courage to speak out in their deep commitment to the core values of the organization. Even when labeled traitors by their colleagues, such tellers of unsettling truths often feel passionate loyalty to the organization and act because they feel the secret activity violates its mission and ethical core.

While we believe leaders must set the example for their organizations by demanding candor and transparency, current leaders have less and less choice in the matter. In today's world, where information travels globally with the click of a mouse, transparency is no longer simply desirable, it is becoming unavoidable.

Many leaders continue to act as if they can hold awkward or damaging truths so close that the outside world will not learn of them. Those days are over. The rise of the blog has transformed the very idea of transparency. There was a time when the worst thing that could happen to an organization with nasty secrets was the emergence of a determined and credible insider with the ear of a respected journalist. But with the rise of blogs, the once vulnerable and isolated whistleblower has ready access to an electronic ally with a new set of superpowers. Whistleblowers no longer have to make their case to a reporter or put their career at risk by going public. They can now make their charges anonymously, and when they do, blogs allow the information to be disseminated throughout cyberspace at the speed of light.

It was Lian Yue, for example, who raised the alarm about the proposed chemical plant in Xiamen, China. According to Xiao Qiang, a cyber-editor who runs the China Internet Project at the University of California, Berkeley, Lian is one of 16 million Chinese bloggers with increasing clout despite government efforts to control cyberspace, which include hiring "tens of thousands of personnel . . . to police the Internet." As Xiao wrote in the *Wall Street Journal,* Chinese bloggers feel increasing safety in numbers and have growing public support: "Facing these independent voices, the old ideological machine starts to crumble."[9]

But traditional whistleblowers who live in the wrong country at the wrong time still put their lives at risk. In 2001 Antonio Siba-Siba Macuacua, a bank official in Mozambique, discovered that one of the country's banks was being looted by well-connected citizens, including government officials.[10] Siba-Siba outed them, revealing in the country's leading newspaper the names of more than a thousand people who had taken out loans they never intended to repay. Not long after his explosive revelation, Siba-Siba was thrown to his death down a stairwell in one of the banks he was investigating. His murder has never been solved.

Few modern American whistleblowers have been murdered, the suspicious death of anti-nuclear and labor activist Karen Silkwood in 1976 notwithstanding. And today they are almost certain to be heard, if only by blogging their way to public notice. But the hit-or-miss nature of old-style whistle-blowing could make for heart-stopping drama, as fictionalized in director Sidney Pollack's 1975 thriller, *Three Days of the Condor*. The film's protagonist, played by Robert Redford, works for the Central Intelligence Agency. When his entire department is wiped out, he threatens to go to the *New York Times* to reveal that the C.I.A. has assassinated half a dozen innocent Americans. "How do you know they'll print it?" his superior at the agency asks the would-be whistleblower. Today if the *New York Times* won't print your story, any number of bloggers with far more readers will. As writer Clive Thompson writes in *Fast Company*: "So many blogs rely on scoops to drive their traffic that muckraking has become a sort of mass global hobby."[11]

Ironically, even as whistle-blowing becomes easier because of the Internet, it remains dangerous to one's professional health. Whistleblowers continue to risk losing their jobs and harming their chances of finding another. Although official assurances of transparency have increased, the U.S. Whistleblower Protection Act of 1989 has been seriously weakened in recent years. According to *Mother Jones* magazine, the biggest setback was a 2006 ruling by the U.S. Supreme Court denying public employees certain First Amendment protections when in an official capacity.[12] The court also lessened protections against workplace retaliation.

But in at least one instance the Internet has protected a whistleblower from his enemies. The endangered critic is Indian engineer M. N. Vijayakumar, who has repeatedly exposed corruption among his civil-service colleagues in the state of Karnataka. In the past, a number of Indian whistleblowers have been found murdered after making similar charges. But according to the *New York Times*, the whistleblower's wife, J. N. Jayashree, has come up with a high-tech, highly original way to keep her husband safe. With the help of their college-student son, she has started a blog devoted to Vijayakumar.[13] She reasons that as long as the electronic light remains on her husband, he is safe. "We're creating a fortress around him—a fortress of people," she said of her husband's digital sanctuary. "I wanted to inform people that this is happening, that my husband is a whistleblower, so that it becomes the responsibility of every citizen to protect him."

TRANSPARENCY, READY OR NOT

According to *Fortune* magazine, 23,000 new blogs appeared online every day in early 2005.[14] By mid-2007, there were an estimated 70 million blogs in the clumsily named blogosphere, up from 15,000 in 2002. Many of these are focused on a particular industry, organization, or interest group and are able to tap well-informed inside sources eager to leak information without revealing their identities and putting their relationships or jobs at risk. And blogs can do far more than reveal secrets. They are able to spread information virally at stunning speed. In contrast to most mainstream media, which strive to present both sides, many blogs openly reflect a particular point of view, including both political liberalism and conservatism. Perhaps as a result of their upfront partisanship, blogs often trigger and reinforce strong emotional responses in readers. They also provide those readers with ways to act on their feelings. Conservative political bloggers famously helped undermine John Kerry's bid for the presidency of the United States in 2002 and brought a tarnished end to the career of Dan Rather, when bloggers accused the veteran broadcaster of using tainted documents about President George Bush's spotty National Guard service.

Blogs can blindside and cause damage to companies as well as individuals. As the same *Fortune* piece points out, in September 2004, a cyclist revealed on a specialty Web site that popular Kryptonite bicycle locks could be opened with a Bic pen.[15] Within hours, videos showing how to pick the locks appeared on several blogs. Although the mainstream media (so despised and yet increasingly emulated by bloggers) picked up the story a few days later, the blog version was seen by 1.8 million people. Faced with this electronic tsunami, Kryptonite announced little more than a week later that it would replace the flawed locks. The estimated cost? Ten million dollars—almost half of the company's projected earnings for the year.

No leader can afford to ignore such a force. Even when damaging information is first revealed by the traditional media, the public's emotional response seems to be heightened somehow in the blogosphere. Economically lethal boycotts can be launched in seconds through blogs. The primary reason for not releasing a dangerous product, such as iatrogenic Vioxx or Guidant's defective defibrillators, should, of course, be a moral one. But every leader needs to keep in mind that the blogosphere is always there, waiting, watching, opining, and persuading. Blogs are uniquely powerful tools for promoting products, brands, and ideas, but they can also be ruthless and all but unstoppable in punishing what they disapprove of. And as their numbers soar, blogs will only get more powerful.

One reason blogs are so effective is that they can be written and read anywhere by anyone with computer access. Blogs and other electronic media also have far greater reach than their traditional rivals. As the University of Southern California's Jonathan Taplin told attendees at a Canadian conference on Internet issues, a popular video on YouTube recently got 9 million hits. In contrast, a successful cable television program attracts about 800,000 viewers.[16] Blogs exist in a cyberworld of more than a billion Internet users, a universe without national borders serving, and creating, a community whose sole bond is the shared desire to participate. Governments have yet to figure out how to control this vast, ever-changing digital community, try as they may. Thus, as China-watcher Xiao points out, China can mobilize tens of thousands of cybercops to police its millions of bloggers, but no wall is great enough to silence them.

Bloggers have the ability, previously limited to comic-book superheroes, to leap national borders in a single bound. In 2005, for example, the *New York Times* reported on the impact a Minnesota blogger was having on Canadian politics.[17] Circumventing a "publication ban" ordered by a Canadian federal judge, the American blogger was reporting testimony being given in a Toronto courtroom about alleged corruption of Canadian Liberal Party officials. Because of the judge's order, Canadian newspapers were not permitted to report the testimony themselves; instead, they told their readers about the existence of the blog. As a result, Canadians began accessing the Minneapolis-based blog and getting their news that way. The blogger—Edward Morrissey—called the phenomenon "a historic moment for blogs," and rightfully so, since his Captain's Quarters blog was able to give Canadians the transparency their own court would have denied them. "The point of having free speech and a free press is to have people informed," Morrissey said. "These information bans are self-defeating for free societies. The politicians know, the media knows, but the Canadian voters are left in the dark and that's a backwards way of doing things."

Leaders would do well to take what Mr. Morrissey said to heart. The leaders who will thrive and whose organizations will flourish in this era of ubiquitous electronic tattle-tales are the ones who strive to make their organizations as transparent as possible. Despite legitimate moral and legal limits on disclosure, leaders should at least aspire to a policy of "no secrets." The first beneficiaries of such a policy are the members of the organization itself, who are in a position to act on maximum rather than restricted information. According to *Fast Company* magazine, Whole Foods CEO John Mackey has a "no secrets" policy that includes posting every employee's pay.[18] The rationale for this and other egalitarian and transparency-related practices (including limiting executive pay to a modest multiple of everyone else's) is Mackey's belief in the "shared fate" of all who work at Whole Foods. Transparency is a highly valued element in the Whole Foods culture, and likely a contributing factor in its frequent appearance at the top of lists of best places to work.

Even if unattainable, a "no secrets" policy is worth striving for. Given that secrecy and even privacy are less and less likely in a world where every teenager has a cell phone equipped with a camera and Internet access, we all need to remember that each of us is, more or less, always under scrutiny and on display. To forget that is to risk embarrassment or worse. Best to do or say nothing that you might have to apologize for if it makes headlines or is reported in a blog. Whether we like it or not, the new, involuntary transparency calls for a new code of behavior, one dictated by the reality that we can never assume we are alone or unwatched. However unwanted this new exposure, it is increasingly a fact of life. You are not safe even in your own home. There are now real estate blogs that document life in individual neighborhoods, complete with videos of locals who wander nude through their houses without closing the blinds.[19]

Ironically, among those who learned the hard way that secrets are harder to keep than ever is transparency advocate John Mackey. In July 2007, the media revealed that the Whole Foods founder and CEO had been using a pseudonym to make controversial posts to an online stock forum. Using the handle Rahodeb, an anagram of Deborah (his wife's name), Mackey had been promoting Whole Foods and slamming rival Wild Oats, even as Whole Foods was in the process of acquiring the smaller firm.[20] Although the takeover was finally approved, Mackey's deception provided ammunition to the Federal Trade Commission, which had filed an antitrust action against the acquisition.

Mackey's online masquerade was, in the words of one former Securities and Exchange Commission official, "bizarre and ill-advised, even if it isn't illegal." Just how bizarre? When not railing against Wild Oats and boosting Whole Foods, Rahodeb once cooed about his own haircut as pictured in a Whole Foods annual report: "I think he looks cute!" Why post as Rahodeb? "Because I had fun doing it," Mackey said. Perhaps because he was known as a maverick before the Rahodeb affair, Mackey seems to have survived the incident without harming his pricey natural foods chain or permanently damaging his own reputation. Digitally savvy critics scornfully labeled him a sock puppet (someone who pretends to be someone else online and then praises himself), but several employees at a local Whole Foods said they accepted his apology on the firm's Web site. However, it is worth noting how long Mackey was able to maintain his deception. He posted on the Yahoo site for almost eight years, until 2006. That Mackey was able to disguise his true identity for so long is a cautionary reminder that, while the Internet has dramatically accelerated the trend toward transparency, it can still conceal as well as reveal—often for a very long time.

When Mackey was exposed, he quickly turned to the firm's Web site to apologize to employees and shareholders for what he acknowledged was inappropriate behavior. Internet-savvy executives know to reach quickly for the Send key to explain themselves in a crisis. As Clive Thompson shrewdly observes in his *Fast Company* piece "The See-Through CEO": "Google is not a search engine. Google is a reputation-management system." No one is more aware of the truth of that statement than Apple's Steve Jobs, who helped create the digital world we all now live in. He quickly went into crisis-management mode in September 2007, turning to the firm's Web site to appease Apple loyalists outraged when he slashed the price of the $600 iPhone just two months after they had stood in line for hours to be the first to have it. Customer blogs suggest that most accepted Jobs's online admission that the price cut was a mistake and his offer of a rebate on future purchases at Apple stores. Less digitally adept executives need to have surrogates in place who understand the blogosphere better than they do and who can respond at blog-speed to developing crises.

The best companies will have thought through, even practiced, how to deal with such emergencies before they happen, not after. As a rule, genuine leaders who encourage the honest sharing of information create organizations that have reputations for candor. Able to draw on public good will, such organizations tend to weather scrutiny more easily when things go wrong. Such leaders tend to respond in ways that maintain their clients' trust and respect even in the face of a disappointing action, product, or policy. Their organizations have little to fear from bloggers, especially when leaders acknowledge mistakes in a timely fashion instead of waiting for outsiders to discover them.

IMPEDIMENTS TO TRANSPARENCY

In a rational universe, organizations and individuals would embrace transparency on both ethical and practical grounds, as the state in which it is easiest to accomplish one's goals. But that is rarely the case. Even as global forces tug us toward greater openness, powerful countervailing forces tend to stymie candor and transparency. Since many of these forces are unconscious and reflect deep-seated human fears and desires, it is worth looking at them more closely.

First, leaders often routinely mishandle information, setting a bad example for the entire group. A common malady among organizational insiders is hoarding information. This is one of many ways information gets stuck in organizations and is kept from flowing to those who need it to make solid decisions. As Wood notes in his analysis of how recent presidents have treated sensitive information, one result of wholesale classification is to keep information away from the frontline staff actually doing the people's business. (Classification also stymies oversight, Graeme notes.) One reason for the hoarding of information by a small clique of insiders is the all-too-human tendency to want to know things that others do not. Some executives seem to take an almost juvenile pleasure in knowing the organization's inside dope and keeping it away from their underlings. In many organizations, knowledge is viewed as the ultimate executive perk, not unlike the company jet, kept solely for the use and delight of the organizational elite. This stance can be costly in terms of both organizational efficiency and morale.

Second, structural impediments often hamper information flow. A now-classic case of how the very design of an organization can hamper good decision making occurred in America's intelligence community. As with so many instances of bungled decision making, this one only came to light after a disaster: the revelation that the United States had declared war on Iraq largely on the basis of seriously flawed data.

Subsequent internal investigations brought a structural problem to light; inadvertently, the system of information flow had been designed to foster poor decisions by depriving key decision makers of crucial data. The main organizational flaw lay in the different mandates of two divisions at the Central Intelligence Agency: the operations directorate, which gathers intelligence data from around the world, and the intelligence directorate, which sifts through that raw information to draw conclusions.[21]

To protect the identities of their sources, the operations people did not reveal to the analysts their own internal assessments of the reliability of the source of a given piece of data. As a result, sources with low credibility introduced into the mix information that only later was found to be wrong. Had the intelligence directorate known what the operations directorate knew about the unreliability of some Iraqi sources, it would have concluded that Iraq had no weapons of mass destruction, that Iraq had no connection to Al Qaeda, and that it had no active nuclear weapons program. But government decision makers, oblivious to the unreliability of the data, took the supposed facts at face value. The subsequent postmortem resulted in proposals for a redesign of information procedures at the C.I.A. The biggest lesson for the C.I.A. was simple: analysts were no longer to be put in the position of making a judgment on crucial issues without full understanding of the reliability and source of the relevant information.

Businesses, though, tend to operate with less openness about mistakes—and fewer full-scale investigations—than does a democratic government, and so examples from government are easier to find than from corporations. But any time an organization makes a seriously wrong decision, its leaders should call for an intensive postmortem. Such learning opportunities are too often overlooked. The tendency is simply to call on the public relations department to spin the matter, to make another inadequately thought-out decision, and perhaps to scapegoat, even fire, a few staff members. Because most companies cover up their mistakes instead of learning from them, systemic flaws in information flow tend to remain to do their damage another day.

A major pharmaceutical company was the rare exception. The company had prospered and grown over the years by acquiring smaller firms. But one promising-looking acquisition went surprisingly awry. The acquired company had had close to 90 percent of its market. Just one year after the firm was acquired, its market share had fallen by more than 60 percent. Seeing those figures, the corporation's CEO wisely mandated an internal review.

That review revealed a flaw in the process of choosing those charged with integrating newly acquired companies into the larger corporation. Choosing someone for that crucial task was typically left to executives who looked at the business expertise of a small pool of candidates, and then chose the most likely person. But in studying what went wrong with this particular acquisition, the CEO learned that the selection process had neglected the steadily growing body of expertise Human Resources had developed on precisely which abilities made an executive a successful integration manager. The most effective integrations had been led by people who possessed such competencies as empathy and the ability to foster teamwork. Newly acquired companies whose integration managers lacked those qualities were far more likely to founder. As a result, HR now plays an active role in choosing integration managers at the pharmaceutical firm.

The so-called shimmer factor is a third common impediment to the free flow of information. The very public and precipitous fall of so many celebrity CEOs has dimmed the once-shining image of executives to some degree. But despite the discrediting of Enron executives, among others, leaders still tend to be perceived by many as demigods. And that perception still deters followers from telling those leaders essential but awkward truths. As everyone who has ever worked in an office knows, there is a far different standard for scrutiny of the CEO's expense account from that of a file clerk. In too many, if not most, organizations, one of the privileges of rank is a tendency to get automatic approval of behavior that would be questioned in the less exalted. Many leaders encourage this godlike view of themselves in countless nonverbal ways, from the cost and spotlessness of their desks to the size and isolation of their homes.

Again and again, we hear tales of leaders who do something outrageous, undeterred by those who should be watching but who fail to speak up because the leader is so daunting. A classic example was that of the Hollinger International board, which okayed, apparently without asking hard questions, the purchase for $8 million of papers relating to Franklin Delano Roosevelt for then-CEO Conrad Black. The only evidence of the value of the collection, which Lord Black sought for a biography of FDR he was writing, was an appraisal by the seller. Hardly a disinterested party, the seller claimed the collection had tripled in value in less than a year. As to why the board was so quick to rubber-stamp the purchase, according to the *New York Times*, "several people close to the board . . . insist that it was not negligence, but something more like awe, that accounts for the free rein Lord Black was given."[22] Black was apparently trusted, even admired, by Henry Kissinger and the rest of the board, so much so that it failed to remember its obligation to the company's stockholders to scrutinize Black's behavior. As one governance expert put it, the board failed in its "duty of curiosity."[23]

It is not clear what might have overcome the board's dazzled acceptance of Black's behavior and allowed it to question the transaction and other corporate misconduct. At the least the board should have acted in the spirit of the old saw, "You trust your mother but you cut the cards." The board's reputation was seriously tarnished by the matter, and indeed the objectivity of boards as a whole was widely questioned in the wake of the Black scandal. As for Black himself, in late 2007 he was found guilty in a U.S. federal court on three counts of fraud and one of obstruction of justice and sentenced to six and a half years in prison.

The best antidote to the shimmer effect is the behavior of the leader. The wisest leaders seek broad counsel, not because they are so enlightened but because they need it. Power does not confer infallibility. There's a compelling reason to become more open to information from people at every level: those close to the action usually know more about what's actually going on with clients, with production or customer service, than do those on the top floors. (There's truth to the maxim, "None of us is as smart as all of us.") Effective leaders find their own ways to elicit many points of view. The CEO of a Pacific Rim bank, for instance, schedules twenty days each year to meet with groups of his top eight hundred people, forty at a time. Aware that isolation in a corner office may weaken his ability to make good decisions, he seeks frank feedback from many sources on a regular basis.

But leaders have to do more than ask for the counsel of others. They have to hear it. All of us would do well to reflect on how receptive we are to the suggestions and opinions of others and alternate points of view. One motive for turning a deaf ear to what others have to say seems to be sheer hubris: leaders often believe they are wiser than all those around them. The literature on executive narcissism tells us that the self-confidence top executives need can easily blur into a blind spot, an unwillingness to turn to others for advice. Kevin Sharer, CEO of Amgen, keeps a cautionary portrait of General George Custer in his office to remind himself of the dangers of overestimating his leadership ability. And Sharer commissioned a portrait of Horatio Nelson to add to his office gallery, after reading a biography of the English naval hero and learning of his genius for collaborative decision making and consensus building.[24]

In extreme cases, narcissism can lead people at the top to refuse to hear what others say. Leaders in such organizations suffer from what some in the Middle East call "tired ears." The CEO of one international organization, for instance, decried the lack of an informal pipeline within the company—he felt that the executive summaries he received daily from his direct reports were being sanitized for him. Yet he could not imagine himself turning to anyone lower in the ranks for a private conversation—let alone cultivating a nonpowerful confidant—because it might be seen as a sign of weakness on his part.

One of the dirty little secrets of many organizations is a debilitating caste system that identifies a few as stars, who are then rewarded and afforded special privileges, and damns the rest as mediocrities who are expected to be good little soldiers who work hard and keep their mouths shut. Some call this the "Golden Boy" syndrome. Many at the top seek counsel only from this leader-anointed A-team. It is hard to say why such organizational hierarchies develop, although one reason is surely that the golden boys and girls, whatever their other limitations, have the ability to please those above them in the organization. Leaders need to question their willingness to hear certain voices and not others. They need to make a habit of second-guessing their enthusiasms as well as their antipathies, since both can cloud their judgment. There is also a strong case to be made for democratizing the workplace and minimizing stratification. In idea-driven organizations—and which are not these days?—genuine, collegial collaboration leads to better morale, a greater likelihood of creativity, and greater candor and transparency. The more everyone knows and the more equally everyone is treated, the more likely it is that everyone will share the truth as he or she sees it. Greater collegiality lubricates the process of information sharing.

INTERNAL TRANSPARENCY

One obvious value of transparency is that it helps keep organizations honest by making more members aware of organizational activities. That is no small virtue. But an equally compelling reason for organizational candor is that it maximizes the probability of success. We are not even talking here about the reality, still not fully absorbed by many leaders, that any organizational failing is more likely to be exposed these days by digital technology. Rather we are talking about the enormous value of internal transparency. There may have been a time when an imperial leader could know everything an organization needed to know to be successful. But if such a time ever existed, it is long gone. Today, the information an organization needs may be located anywhere, including outside. And the leader who has a narrow view of proper channels for information often pays a high price for its orderly but insufficient flow.

A universal problem is that when staff speak to their leader, the very nature of the message tends to change. The message is likely to be spun, softened, and colored in ways calculated to make it more acceptable to the person in power. In order to continue to receive reliable information, those in power must be aware that whatever they hear from their direct reports has probably been heavily edited, if only to make the message more palatable and to make the messenger appear more valuable. And so wise leaders find ways to get information raw. They solicit and embrace the bad news as well as the good. Among the leaders acutely aware of the need to get unbiased information was George Washington. According to David Hackett Fischer's *Washington's Crossing,* Washington solicited intelligence from as many people as possible, even civilians, before going into battle. Washington seems to have had an intuitive grasp of the dangers of the shimmer effect (and few, even among the founding fathers, shimmered as dazzlingly as he did) and its tendency to make subordinates compliant. As Fischer writes: "It was typical of Washington's leadership to present a promising proposal as someone else's idea, rather than his own. It was his way of encouraging open discussion and debate."[25]

How differently then U.S. Secretary of Defense Donald Rumsfeld behaved early in 2003 in the face of informed intelligence he apparently did not want to hear. When asked by a member of the Senate Armed Services Committee how large a force would be needed in postwar Iraq, General Eric Shinseki spoke frankly and said, "Something on the order of several hundred thousand soldiers are probably . . . a figure that would be required."[26] Wrong answer, in the view of Rumsfeld and others in the administration who claimed (incorrectly, as it turned out) that peace could be maintained in Iraq with a minimum of ground forces. Shinseki, who chose a military career despite being seriously wounded in the Vietnam War, had served with distinction for more than thirty-five years, including a stint as U.S. Army chief of staff. But as Bill Clinton observed, Shinseki "committed candor." As a result, he was publicly criticized by Defense Department officials, and Rumsfeld and other luminaries boycotted his retirement ceremony. For whatever reasons, Rumsfeld chose not to know all that he should have.

The classic example of a leader's apparently willful blindness is Shakespeare's Julius Caesar. He refused to read the signs of impending doom that were everywhere on the Ides of March, including his wife's dream of a statue of Caesar spurting blood.

Moments before his enemies drew their knives, he literally refused to read the last-ditch warning put in his hand by a loyal follower.

Other factors can also distort information flow. The need for speed—more pressing now than ever—also militates against the systematic collection and analysis of information, as does the need for the organization, and especially its leader, to look decisive. Indeed one of the most dangerous myths of modern organizations is that it is better to make a bad decision than no decision. Instead of mythologizing the leader who acts quickly or on hunches, we should cultivate leaders who are not afraid to be labeled wishy-washy when prudent caution and additional study are called for. Action in the absence of good intelligence can be a terribly expensive course, and precipitous leadership is more likely to be reckless than a sign of strength. There is a tendency, especially in the management literature that equates risk-taking with learning, to downplay the real cost of failures and other actions that go awry, perhaps because the full price is almost never paid by the decision makers themselves. It is rarely possible, in today's world, to defer action until everything relevant is known and everyone who will be impacted is engaged. But both adequate knowledge and full disclosure, if not consensus, are worthwhile goals that enhance transparency and tip the balance toward a successful outcome.

Sunken costs are another common obstacle to changing course and to greater transparency. Even more insidious are the negative consequences that can arise in an enthusiastically shared mission. Again and again, we see organizations that blind themselves to institutional flaws and even crimes because they are intoxicated with ambition. The drive to succeed, to be No. 1, can be a giddy race in which the normal moral machinery breaks down. Commitment can inspire an organization and pervert it at the same time. History is littered with examples. On a more mundane level, a marketing executive at a highly successful memory storage company confided to us that its services were so highly valued that salespeople routinely inflated charges to customers. The executive thought the practice was not only wrong but ultimately bad for business: he believed such gouging might boost the company's bottom line for a time but would inevitably backfire once customers realized they were being cheated. The executive had grave doubts about the practice, which was an open secret among the sales force. But his own boss, the head of marketing, was so proud of his sales force—and the short-term boost their dishonesty was giving the company's stock price—that the troubled executive was afraid to pass along the nasty truth. The company's aggressive can-do credo—especially in sales—kept the executive from speaking up, allowing the dishonesty to continue.

A dangerous tendency toward silence may be an accepted but unspoken value of an entire discipline, not just a particular organization. For example, in a paper on factors that silence conflict, Harvard Business School professors Leslie Perlow and Nelson Repenning cite research among automotive industry engineers that found "a basic cultural commandment in engineering—don't tell someone you have a problem unless you have a solution."[27] Such unspoken professional rules may have a profound impact on how an organization functions. We can't help but wonder, for instance, if the lack of a ready solution was what prompted NASA to okay both the tragic *Challenger* and *Columbia* shuttle flights in spite of staff misgivings about the former's O-rings and the latter's foam insulation. Implicit values may be so entrenched that they are never fully uncovered, even in the course of an extensive inquiry following a tragic accident.

In most organizations, hidden ground rules govern what can be said and what cannot. One key question that every leader should ask to encourage candor: Is it safe to bring bad news to those at the top? The first time a top executive blows up or punishes someone delivering bad news, a norm is established. Everyone quickly realizes that it is folly to speak unwanted truth to power, no matter how crucial the information may be (more on speaking truth to power in Essay Two). Leaders must show that speaking up is not just safe but mandatory, and that no information of substance is out of bounds. It is not always easy for even the most confident leaders to embrace hard truths, especially when they are presented awkwardly by someone who is neither a friend nor a trusted colleague. But failing to hear critical information, whoever delivers it, may put the entire enterprise at risk.

A few thousand businesses have decided to mechanize transparency by installing so-called whistleblower software. Offered by such companies as EthicsPoint and Global Compliance Services, the software allows employees to report anonymously to management any suggestions, complaints, concerns about safety or other matters, and evidence of wrongdoing.[28] Some systems also send any complaint about the CEO or other key executives to a member of the board for further inquiry. Publicly traded companies can point to the software as evidence that the firm is meeting its obligation under the Sarbanes-Oxley Act of 2002 to establish mechanisms for identifying corporate transgressions.

A senior vice president told *Inc.* magazine that his privately held Minnesota company had installed an electronic whistle-blowing system because "we want to demonstrate that we are serious about establishing an ethical culture." Only about 3 percent of employee complaints uncovered major problems, *Inc.* reports. But proponents say they value the systems for alerting them to potential problems while they are still in-house. The systems have also saved users money by limiting losses related to fraud and other wrongdoing.

OPACITY BEGINS AT HOME

Although some enlightened organizations opt for openness, many more are characterized by blind spots and black holes that prevent the free flow of information and impede candor. Why? We have to look to the dynamics of family life for the first, most powerful, model for what we notice and how we think about it. The rules we learn as family members teach us what we should pay attention to, and how we should speak about what we notice. Every family tacitly teaches each member four attentional rules:

- These are the things we notice.

- This is what we say about them.

- These are the things we don't notice.

- And we never say anything to outsiders about that third category.

The last two rules lead to the creation of family secrets. Danish playwright Henrik Ibsen coined the term "vital lies" for the operative fictions that cover a more disturbing truth in troubled families. A vital lie masks a truth that is too threatening, dangerous, or painful to be spoken aloud. The vital lie preserves the surface harmony of the family but at great cost. Problems that are not acknowledged rarely get better on their own.[29]

A similar dynamic afflicts many organizations. For instance, at one global company, the new head of HR bemoaned the fact that her predecessor presided over an evaluation system that rated every executive as "excellent," even as the company was losing a quarter billion dollars a year. The vital lie that all the company's leaders were top-notch wallpapered over their palpable shortcomings; it didn't make them go away. Ultimately, continued losses forced the company to confront the fiction of its great leadership. In the turnaround that followed, virtually every one of its "excellent" leaders was replaced.

The emotion that seals people's lips about vital lies is the unconscious fear that if we look at and speak about these dangerous secrets, we will either destroy the family or be expelled from it. The anxiety of living with these secrets is often allayed by ignoring them.

To be sure, not all family secrets are bad. There are "sweet secrets" that have a bonding effect, like the private terms of endearment used within families. The dangers lie in toxic or dangerous secrets, like the fact that a mother is alcoholic and neglects her children, that a visiting uncle was once jailed for sexually abusing children, or that a family fortune has its roots in criminal acts.

When as adults we join an organization, we bring our earlier learning about how to be part of a family into the "corporate family." Without anyone having to explicitly tell us how things are, we automatically learn what to notice and what to think and say about it. We also learn what to ignore— and we already know from childhood not to speak about the things we know not to notice. The fears in work life echo those from family life: if we speak the unspeakable, we may threaten the organization itself, or risk expulsion. Everyone in an organization has experience in keeping secrets—for better or for worse.

But more positive forces are at work here, too. Pride in belonging to a high-performing or high-status group and the cozy sense of belonging to a tight-knit organizational "family" can be genuine sources of professional satisfaction. The paradox is that there is a dark side to belonging—the almost reflexive temptation to spin information in ways that protect the group's shared pride, to make the group look better than it really is, or even simply to preserve the group. All these make it easier for group members to suppress information or distort it.

In the world of work, conspiracies of silence are enormously damaging and all but universal. We have all worked in places where no one addressed the problem that everyone knew about: the office bully no one confronts; the budget games, where people skew numbers and exaggerate expectations; the board of directors that tacitly suppresses dissent to support a charismatic CEO; the arrogant doctor who makes mistakes nurses see but are afraid to point out.

For instance, Harvard Business School's Leslie Perlow studied an office equipment company where vast amounts of time were devoted to weekly meetings.[30] Before sitting down with the boss each week, the company's software engineers took time that might have been better spent on meaningful work preparing impressive presentations. The engineers thought the meetings were a huge waste of time, but none of them dared speak up, believing management wanted the meetings. Ironically, the engineers' boss also thought the meetings had little value. But as Perlow told the *New York Times,* the boss didn't want to cancel the gatherings because he thought it would send the message that he didn't value the work of the engineers. What Perlow calls "the vicious spiral of silence" undermined both productivity and morale.

The vital lies of organizations show remarkable similarities to those of families. Take an example from family life, where the mother is an alcoholic, and the other adult relatives are co-dependents who tacitly facilitate her behavior. The mother often starts drinking before noon and can no longer function by late afternoon. Instead of speaking about her addiction, other family members say she's "had a nip" and is now not passed out but "taking a nap." Just as troubled families do, companies and other organizations often find ways to talk about their guilty secrets in coded, euphemistic language that outsiders won't understand. The C.I.A.'s use of the cozy term "family jewels" for evidence of assassination attempts and other dark deeds is one example. Another surfaced in the court testimony about wrongdoing by the finance department at HealthSouth.[31] The company's accounting and finance specialists actually referred to themselves as "the family," even as they concocted phony business deals to meet soaring earnings expectations. The corporate conspirators referred to the gap between the company's actual quarterly earnings and Wall Street's expectations as "the hole." They called the deals they dreamed up to fill that hole "dirt." Just as in families, organizational secrets distort relationships. Those sharing the secret tend to form a more tightly knit bond while distancing themselves from outsiders, thus cutting themselves off from those who might expose them as well as those who might influence them in positive ways. Many of the corporate scandals of recent years appear to have been perpetrated by insiders who shared real camaraderie until they realized the only way to save themselves from prison sentences was to turn on each other.

STOPPING GROUPTHINK

As we have found again and again, one of the dangerous ironies of leadership is that those at the top often think they know more than they do. There seems to be an inexorable filtering out of bad news that often leaves those in the highest positions with potentially disastrous information gaps. Our research, for instance, shows that the higher leaders rise, the less honest feedback they get from followers about their leadership. Direct reports understandably hesitate to enumerate the boss's leadership failings. And so top leaders easily lose touch with the ways others see them and may remain poor listeners, abrasive, tuned out, or otherwise clueless about their own limitations.

The routine keeping of accurate information from the leader may lead to *groupthink* in decision making.[32] The classic groupthink case, described by Yale psychologist Irving Janis, was John F. Kennedy's 1962 decision to invade Cuba at the Bay of Pigs. For months before the invasion, JFK met daily with a tight-knit, fiercely proud group of top advisers—heads of intelligence, the military, and the State Department—who assured him that their intelligence reports showed that an armed underground of Cubans would rise up against Castro to support the invaders. No one brought up the results of a careful poll, done the year before, that showed the vast majority of

Cubans supported Castro. No one paid attention to the dissenting opinions of the highly informed experts on the State Department Cuba desk. Another key assumption was that if the Bay of Pigs invasion faltered, the invading army could retreat to the nearby Escambray Mountains and hold out there. No one seemed aware that the Bay of Pigs was eighty miles from the safety of the Escambray Mountains.[33]

And so it went for weeks: crucial facts that dictated a "no" decision on the invasion were edited out of the discussion, though each one of these facts was known by one or more people sitting at the table. When the Bay of Pigs invasion turned into an epic fiasco, Kennedy, stunned, asked, "How could I have been so stupid to let them go ahead?" The unspoken answer was that his best advisers had collectively and unwittingly led him into the disaster.

Whenever a tight-knit decision-making group fails to collect all relevant data and candidly analyze it, bad decisions are liable to be made. The Bay of Pigs has its echo today in the ill-fated decision of another tight-knit, fiercely proud presidential advisory group, one whose unquestioned assumptions now resemble vital lies: that Saddam Hussein was conspiring with Al Qaeda, that Iraq harbored a trove of weapons of mass destruction, that the Iraqi people would rise up to embrace a liberating army.

Those assumptions are part of a new textbook case of groupthink, the failure of the C.I.A. to provide reliable evaluations of Iraq's weapons and armed forces in the run-up to the second Iraq War. The subsequent congressional investigation made an explicit diagnosis of groupthink—a process in which unfounded assumptions drive a plan of action and contradictory information is suppressed, along with any doubts about the assumptions themselves.[34] For instance, one claim made in support of a preemptive war against Iraq was that it had mapping software for use inside the United States.[35] That claim was paired with the unfounded assumption that Iraq had weapons of mass destruction to suggest Iraq was planning an attack with such weapons on the United States. The C.I.A. did not reveal that the mapping software was an innocuous component of a larger generic software package for the guidance of drones.

Groupthink-driven decisions are the downside of a dynamic every organization seeks to build: group cohesiveness and pride in belonging. The paradox here is that the very cohesiveness that can make such tight-knit groups highly effective can shade over into a clubby sense of entitlement and superiority. This can lead members to believe that the group can do no wrong—that stretching rules to achieve its goals is, for them, permissible. Just such overweening in-group pride was at play in many of the regrettable corporate scandals of recent years. For this reason, the CEO of a major investment bank recommended to us that companies transfer leaders every five years or so to limit their power and that of their teams.

Genuine leaders learn from their mistakes, including having been blindsided by groupthink. For JFK, the Bay of Pigs was a searing lesson in how not to lead. Freshly aware of how groupthink could subvert the decision-making process, Kennedy demanded his advisers' principled dissent during the Cuban missile crisis in 1962. Kennedy's management of that thirteen-day crisis was a legendary example of a leader drawing the best from multiple advisers and making his decision only after weighing each of their very different contributions.[36] Robert Kennedy later recalled: "The fact that we were able to talk, debate, argue, disagree, and then debate some more was essential in choosing our ultimate course"—a course that averted an international nuclear war.

When Clark Clifford replaced Robert McNamara as Secretary of Defense during the Vietnam War, Clifford abandoned his predecessor's policy of listening only to his direct reports and began talking to people at every level of the department. Clifford felt it was the only way to hear something new and potentially useful.[37] Years later, former Medtronic CEO Bill George said it was his experience in the inbred McNamara Defense Department that made him insist that his Medtronic managers not try to spin and sugarcoat the information they gave him. George said he had to counter a corporate culture of "Minnesota nice" to get his staff to abandon their habit of polite agreement in favor of productive candor. He called it "constructive conflict" and admitted it came hard to many of his Medtronic staff.

CULTIVATING CANDOR

Before an organization can develop a culture of candor, it must examine the cultural rules that currently govern it. Such cultural rules run deep, and they typically resist change. At NASA, for example, the cultural ground rules that contributed to the

Challenger explosion sixteen years before were still operating in 2003, leading to the *Columbia* shuttle disaster. The panel that investigated the causes of the *Columbia* tragedy went beyond the technical cause—a chunk of flyaway foam that damaged a wing—to blame an organizational culture where engineers were afraid to raise safety concerns with managers more worried about meeting flight schedules than about risks.[38] Head of NASA Sean O'Keefe said in the aftermath of the *Columbia* tragedy that no employee who speaks up about safety concerns, even to outsiders, would be reprimanded in any way. But since 2003, NASA has become even less transparent as a result of pressure put on political appointees to the agency to keep employees, including a NASA scientist concerned about global warming, from publicly expressing views not in keeping with current administration policies.

The best way for leaders to start information flowing freely in their organizations is to set a good example. They must accept, even welcome, unsettling information. If leaders regularly demonstrate that they want to hear more than incessant happy talk, and praise those with the courage to articulate unpleasant truths, then the norm will begin to shift toward transparency.

Transparency is one evidence of an organization's moral health. We have come to think that governments, organizations, and other institutions have a kind of DNA. Healthy institutions, including democracy, are more open than unhealthy ones, such as slavery, which fight to keep their ugly secrets. For businesses, openness is not just a virtuous policy that makes the organization feel good about itself, like generous parental leave. Openness and what it says about the nature of the organization becomes a competitive advantage—in creating consumer loyalty as well as in recruiting and keeping the best people. Evidence that values matter to today's consumer include the enormous interest in green products. That values matter to those in the most creative part of the workforce is evidenced by the vast number of people who seek employment at Google, whose motto is famously "Don't be evil."

When we talk about creating a culture of candor, we imply that the organization ultimately has control over the process. Certainly, transparency is enhanced when an organization's leaders are committed to it. But even when leaders resist it, transparency is inescapable in the digital age. The new transparency is not optional. To the evident discomfort of some, recent candidates for the presidency of the United States faced questions during televised debates, not just from participants in time-honored Town Hall forums, but from visitors to the social-networking site YouTube. Used to carefully vetted, controlled encounters, the candidates had to field questions lobbed from cyberspace by cartoon characters and people dressed in goofy costumes. Just as YouTube has changed America's political discourse, Google has made it impossible for any candidate to deny past actions or statements. Within seconds, anyone with a laptop can check on the candidate's past positions and, within a few seconds more, report any distortions or self-serving memory lapses to the entire wired world. Whether the candidates like it or not, a culture of candor has been thrust upon them.

2

JAMES O'TOOLE

SPEAKING TRUTH TO POWER

The truth that makes men free is for the most
part the truth which men prefer not to hear.
—**Herbert Agar**, *A Time for Greatness* (1942)

In 2002, Enron's Sherron Watkins, WorldCom's Cynthia Cooper, and the FBI's Coleen Rowley were recognized as *Time* magazine's "Persons of the Year" for courageously bringing news to the men at the top of their respective organizations that those leaders preferred not to hear. As *Time* reported, the honored trio weren't looking to curry favor, weren't looking for publicity, didn't want to be whistleblowers, and all three—primary breadwinners in their families—courted great risk in terms of their jobs and careers. Sadly, not only did their warnings about serious ethical violations go unheeded by their bosses, the women then were marginalized, isolated, scorned, and reviled by their organizations for their efforts to save them. So why did they dare to speak truth to power? Their motivations differed, but the actions of all three were rooted in what they saw as a moral imperative to act. In the words of Martin Luther King Jr., "Our lives begin to end the day we become silent about things that matter."[1]

Over the next four years, Treasury Secretary Paul O'Neil, counterterrorism expert Richard Clarke, ex-Army chief General Eric K. Shinseki, and White House economic adviser Lawrence Lindsey would suffer fates similar to those of Watkins, Cooper, and Rowley when they dared to speak truth to powerful officials in the administration of President George W. Bush. Indeed, in almost all social organizations—families, sports teams, schools, businesses, government, and nonprofit agencies—those lower down the pecking order experience, from time to time, the terror involved in having to tell unpalatable truths to those ranked above them. While few of us have had direct experience calling attention to Enron-scale fraud and deception, almost all of us have stories to tell of retaliatory fury from the enraged "alpha dogs" we mustered the courage to confront. I once dared to question the factual basis of an assertion Donald Rumsfeld made during a seminar we were attending in the 1990s when he was serving as a corporate executive. He came after me with bone-chilling intensity: "No one questions me! Do you understand that?" And, apparently with total conviction, he added, *"I am never wrong."* Hours after, I was still shaking from the encounter. I learned later that, subsequently, he had tried to get me fired from my job.[2]

Speaking truth to power is, perhaps, the oldest of all ethical challenges. Certainly, it is one of the most terrifying in that it entails personal danger: from the days of the first humans until only relatively recently, tribal leaders, clan elders, kings, tyrants, caudillos, gang leaders, ward bosses, and neighborhood bullies all ruled by force. To question their decisions was to risk death. In the 2006 film *The Last King of Scotland,* a young British doctor is portrayed screwing up his courage to confront Idi Amin, whom he had theretofore loyally served by conveniently turning a blind eye to the dictator's vile acts. Unlike most Ugandans who stood up to Amin, the Scot escapes with his life, but only after suffering unspeakable horrors at the hands of the despot's brutal thugs.

A PROBLEM OF LONG STANDING

The peril of speaking truth to power is a major theme of Sophocles' fourth-century B.C. play *Antigone.* Indeed, the play is the source of the modern cliché "killing the messenger." Early in the action, straws are drawn among King Creon's guards to choose the unlucky one who must tell his majesty that not only has his niece (and soon-to-be daughter-in-law) Antigone defied an edict he has proclaimed but—and far worse in the eyes of the king—the populace is rallying to her support. The losing guard swallows hard, recognizing that "nobody likes the bringer of bad news." Least of all Creon, who greets it first by questioning the guard's loyalty, and then, in a terrifying display of what the Greeks called hubris (the arrogance of power), proclaims that, because he's the king, it is obvious the gods are on his side. American readers of the play can't help but recall Richard Nixon's infamous Watergate defense, "When the President does it, that means it is not illegal."

Creon refuses to listen to Antigone's reasons for defying his edict—she is a woman, after all, and that would be too great a blow to his male ego—as he refuses to hear what the common people have to say, believing that to listen to them would be taken as a sign of weakness and hence constitute a threat to his power. Finally, Creon's son, Haemon, tells his father, "Your presence frightens any common man from saying things you would not care to hear." But the king will brook the truth from no man or woman. Creon stubbornly refuses to listen to anyone and, in the end, brings death to his family, ruin on himself, and destruction to his country.

In *Antigone,* both the messenger and the king face ethically tough choices: the guard is likely to be killed if he speaks truth to power; and, as the king sees it, he must either execute his son's fiancée or undermine his authority to govern. Sophocles implies that the latter choice is both the harder and more morally significant. He puts one lesson of the play in the mouth of the messenger: "To reject good counsel is a crime," and a related moral is stated by a blind seer: "Stubbornness and stupidity are twins."

The history of the following 2,500 years is, alas, replete with tragic examples of powerful men stubbornly rejecting good advice. In fact, the ethical issues and physical perils entailed in speaking truth to power continue today as major themes in modern historical dramas. T.S. Eliot's *Murder in the Cathedral* deals with the events leading to the death of the Archbishop of Canterbury, Thomas à Becket, at the hands of King Henry II's henchmen when Becket places loyalty to the Church above loyalty to his king. Bertolt Brecht's *Galileo Galilei* dramatizes the coercive ways in which the Church of Rome attempted to stifle the great astronomer's scientific proof of a heliocentric solar system. John Osborne's *Luther* portrays the struggles of a single lowly priest against the same powers in Rome at the start of the Reformation. And Robert Bolt's *A Man for All Seasons* concerns the life and death of Thomas Moore, the man Samuel Johnson called "the person of the greatest virtue these islands ever produced." Moore dared to speak truth to Henry VIII ("that monstrous baby whom none dared gainsay") and paid with his life. Loyal to the end to his conscience and, in fact, also to Henry, Moore asks, "Can I help my King by giving him lies when he asks for truth?" At the trial where Moore is sentenced to death, Sir Richard Rich perjures himself to support the King's trumped-up charges. On discovering that Henry had recently appointed Rich to the post of attorney general for Wales, Moore wryly comments: "Why Richard, it profits a man nothing to give his soul for the whole world. . . . But for Wales!"

In sum, these plays stand as reminders to leaders of their ethical duty to create what, in a modern organizational context, my coauthors of this book refer to as transparent "cultures of candor." Significantly, *ethos*, the ancient Greek word for culture (often translated as "character") is also the root of the word *ethics*. In this essay, I illustrate how ethical transparency is predicated on the existence of two parties—a candid speaker of facts and a receptive listener—and how both followers and leaders can benefit from the many historical, literary, and philosophical examples of those who dared speak truth to power.

ANCIENT VALUES APPLIED TODAY

I first read *Antigone* in 1973 and, in the decade that followed, was struck by how often the ethical issues raised by Sophocles in the context of an ancient monarchy were present in the modern corporations where I was doing research and consulting. In 1982, I was invited by the Cowles Media Corporation (owners of the *Minneapolis Star and Tribune*) to meet with its top executives to discuss their corporate culture. I could see why they wanted help: After having lost the magazines *Look* in the 1960s and *Harper's* in the 1970s (the first went belly-up; the second literally had to be given away), the down-in-the-dumps corporation had subsequently seen its net income fall from $12.2 million to $0.7 million between 1979 and 1982. I started the process by asking the top management team for short, descriptive phrases that best described the culture of the company. Silence. I asked again. More silence. Finally, I was passed an unsigned note that read, "Dummy, can't you see that we can't speak our minds? Ask for our input anonymously, in writing." I did so, and for the next two hours I would ask them a question about their culture, they would write down their answers . . . then I would collect them and read the responses back to the group. At the end of this wearying experience, several executives came up to tell me in private that this meeting, which to me had been pathetically sad, was "the best they had had" since John Cowles Jr. had assumed leadership of the corporation! Within a year of the meeting, John Cowles had fired several of those managers for "disloyalty" (for speaking truth to power?) and several others resigned in protest over one or another of his decisions. Shortly thereafter, the Cowles family fired John when the company went into a yet more dire financial tailspin.[3]

But not all the corporations I studied had such toxic cultures. In the late 1970s, I addressed then-start-up Federal Express Corporation's management team on the subject of worker productivity. I had gotten no more than ten minutes into my talk when a young manager interrupted and posed a challenge to his colleagues: "The professor has made an interesting point that runs counter to a major decision management made a couple weeks ago. I suggest we reexamine that decision now in light of what we have just learned." To my amazement, the group picked up the suggestion and turned directly to a no-holds-barred debate of the issue. What really surprised me was that the lower-level managers then made those at the top defend their decision. When it became clear the policy couldn't be defended, the younger managers asked their bosses to change it. Which they did, then and there. This rough-and-tumble exchange lasted for about an hour. At the end, they all went to lunch without a trace of hard feelings, or a sign that anyone had won or lost face, power, or status. Apparently, this openness and willingness to raise tough questions and challenge accepted wisdom was part of the culture of the firm from the start, for I seemed to be the only one in the room who found the exchange unusual. My feeling then, which I expressed in a book in 1985, was that if Federal Express could retain that openness and rare ability to learn and to change, it was a good bet that it would continue to be a remarkable success.

Quite apart from the ethical issues raised by these two contrasting examples, in hindsight, one can see why the Cowles organization ultimately failed to meet the test of sustainability, and why Federal Express went on to become one of the world's most successful global corporations through responding to, and anticipating, technological, social, political, economic, and competitive change. The lesson I drew at the time from these experiences was that managers in companies with healthy cultures are constantly willing to rethink even their most basic assumptions through a process of constructive dissent. And my experience over the next thirty years confirms in my mind that companies get into moral and competitive hot water when their leaders are unwilling to test their operating premises about such often-taboo subjects as the nature of the working conditions they offer employees, the purposes of their corporation, and their responsibilities to various stakeholders.

The failure to openly examine such behavior-driving assumptions leads to what commonly is called *groupthink,* a state of collective denial or self-deception that often has disastrous business and ethical consequences.

While I hesitate to cite the late John Z. DeLorean as an authority on ethical matters, I must acknowledge that he was one of the first business leaders to recognize the consequences of groupthink. In *On a Clear Day You Can See General Motors*, he describes "a typical meeting" of GM's executive committee in which then-chairman Richard Gerstenberg would pontificate and his vice chairman, Richard Terrell ("the master of the paraphrase"), would parrot his views:

> *Gerstenberg:* Goddamnit. We cannot afford any new models next year because of the cost of this federally mandated equipment. There is no goddamn money left for styling changes. That's the biggest problem we face.
>
> *Terrell, after waiting about 10 minutes:* Dick, goddamnit. We've just got to face up to the fact that our number one problem is the cost of this federally mandated equipment. This stuff costs so much that we don't have any money left for styling our new cars. That's our biggest problem.
>
> *Gerstenberg:* You're goddamn right, Dick. That's a good point.

DeLorean clearly was exaggerating, but this hypothetical dialogue usefully illustrates a behavioral problem found in a great many companies. People in organizations typically form shared ideas—"collective representations" in the language of social anthropology—and all the forces of the group conspire to protect those notions, no matter how inaccurate or outmoded they may be, or may become. For example, as the Japanese began to win a share of the U.S. auto market in the late 1970s, DeLorean portrayed GM's top executives in Detroit looking down from their fourteenth-floor executive suite onto the enormous company parking lot below and saying, "Look at all those big cars! Who says Americans want small ones?" Ditto GM's leaders' self-defeating collective representation that American consumers at the time didn't care a fig about product quality.

If only this cultural pattern were confined to the auto industry. But experience shows that, for good or ill, management teams commonly hold shared assumptions about the sources of innovation, motivation, productivity, product quality, and profitability in their respective organizations, and those untested assumptions drive their behavior. Significantly, the more basic— and therefore the more potent—the assumption the *less* likely it is to be examined. Reputedly, the Altria company has squeaky-clean legal compliance procedures thanks to devoting high-level attention and generous resources to their internal auditing and control processes, yet I seriously doubt any of the company's managers could raise the question of the basic morality of its cigarette business. None of us is immune from this phenomenon. We business professors in large research universities resist examining one of the fundamental premises of our enterprise, namely that publishing in "A" journals is the sole measure of scholarly excellence. In truth, all organizations—nations, colleges, businesses, and families—embrace such fundamental and unexamined myths. While such shared values and assumptions play a necessary role in holding a group together, if the glue that binds them is in fact toxic, it can result in organizational morbidity. That's why managers in companies with healthy cultures continually challenge old assumptions, rethink basic premises, question, revise, and unlearn outmoded truths.

An often-told story about Motorola during its heyday in the 1980s concerns a young middle manager who approached then-CEO Robert Galvin: "Bob, I heard that point you made this morning, and I think you are dead wrong. I'm going to prove it. I'm going to shoot you down." The young man stormed off and Galvin, beaming proudly, turned to a shocked companion and said "That's how we've overcome Texas Instruments' lead in semi-conductors!" Significantly, during that same time frame at Motorola there were no rewards for those who supported the status quo: managers got ahead only by challenging existing assumptions, and by proving the fact when they detected imperial nakedness. Galvin would explain to anyone who would listen that he was far from the smartest person at Motorola, and that the company's success was not thanks to him but was, instead, due to the fact that he had surrounded himself with managers more talented than he was. And then he listened to them. Galvin not only made it clear that candor was valued, it was rewarded . . . even if it entailed receiving information he personally found unpleasant. In fact, Galvin put into place a formal process by which the fundamental assumptions of the company were surfaced and then challenged. Unfortunately, over subsequent decades the company lost those good habits.

FOOLS AND SENTRIES

While Motorola failed to do so in the long run, it seems possible to institutionalize the kinds of processes that were dependent upon Galvin's personal leadership. When Verne Morland was an executive at NCR in the 1980s, he suggested that all companies could benefit from hiring a "corporate fool." Like the Fool in Shakespeare's play *King Lear,* the modern organizational equivalent would be a person licensed "To challenge by jest and conundrum all that is sacred and all that the savants have proved to be true and immutable." While this corporate contrarian needn't dress in motley, spangles, and bells, the fool nonetheless would be obligated to "stir up controversy, respect no authority, and resist pressures to engage in detailed analyses." (The need to speak truth to power runs like a leitmotif through Shakespeare's histories and tragedies, as when Hamlet stages his famous play-within-the-play to confront King Claudius with the fact of his hideous crimes: "The play's the thing wherein I'll catch the conscience of the king.")

Who is most willing to play "the fool" in today's organizations? In keeping with William James's observation that "genius . . . means little more than the facility of perceiving in an unhabitual way," consultant Nancy Reeves prophetically suggested in the 1980s that the fool's role—speaking truth to power—might be more natural for women to play than for men because the former "have been outside the status quo ante, and are free to marshal historic exclusions for positive ends. . . .

Women have not learned, and therefore do not have to un-learn, principles no longer pertinent. . . . Women might be the utterers of today's imperative blasphemies." Twenty years later, women in the great tradition of Antigone—Enron's Watkins, WorldCom's Cooper, and the FBI's Rowley—received their due public recognition for having the courage to speak truth to power. In the global realm of politics, where brave people face ostracism, imprisonment, violence, and death in their native countries when defending human rights, fully a third of such brave individuals cited by Kerry Kennedy Cuomo in *Speak Truth to Power* are women.[4]

In general, women seem to exhibit great courage when it comes to standing up for their convictions. While I think this observation can easily be stretched to the breaking point, the percentage of women martyrs seems to be inordinately high among those canonized by the Catholic Church, and history is replete with tales of women who have sacrificed their lives to ensure the safety of their families. In a review of recent developments in the science of evolutionary biology, Robin Marantz Henig describes the role of "sentries," individual birds, meerkats, and members of other animal species who, as "lookouts," put their own lives at risk to protect the overall good of their flocks. Henig says that some humans take "on a role analogous to the sentry bird—a person who stands up to authority, for instance, risks losing his job, going to jail or getting beaten by the police."[5] The question she raises (but doesn't fully answer) is, *Given the high probability of not living to pass on one's genes, what's the evolutionary advantage of being a sentry?*

Perhaps the answer is the existence of a human moral imperative that transcends our biological need to reproduce our DNA.

PERILS OF THE IMPERIUM

While the dangers posed to modern human sentries in the business world are not life threatening, nonetheless the macho behavior of imperial CEOs in the 1990s created a cultural expectation that business leaders need to be decisive, tough, take-charge men who quickly fire those who are not "team players." Imagine the courage it would take to tell a Jack Welch, Scott McNeely, Andy Grove, or Larry Ellison news he didn't want to hear. Even in books written by his admirers, Jack Welch comes across as acting like a bully when GE managers dared to question him.[6] In those accounts, dissenters were said to have been berated, insulted, and abused: "According to former employees, Welch conducts meetings so aggressively that people tremble. He attacks almost physically with his intellect—criticizing, demeaning, ridiculing, humiliating." One former GE executive, who had been publicly dressed down by Welch for daring to question his boss, admitted to the moderator of an Aspen Institute seminar that Welch's furious tirade "caused me to soil my pants."[7]

Perhaps the only thing riskier than telling the boss he is wrong is to have to admit one's own mistakes. Speaking truth to power is a particularly threatening exercise when it entails owning up to serious error. Indeed, fear of punishment by tyrannical leaders causes many managers to become risk averse. To free his people from such crippling fears, Percy Barnevik issued these "General Principles of Management Behavior" when he became CEO of ABB in the 1980s:

> To take action (and stick out one's neck) and do the right things is obviously the best.
>
> To take action and do the wrong things (within reason and a limited number of times) is second best.
>
> Not to take action (and lose opportunities) is the only non-acceptable behavior.[8]

The risks of speaking truth to power are particularly acute for those in professional services firms—the lawyers, accountants, and consultants who are the very gatekeepers charged with providing business leaders with unvarnished assessments and warnings, and with objective advice and counsel. These professionals are too well aware that the fastest way to lose clients is to give them news they don't want to hear. This is especially true when the news that needs conveying is that the client-CEO's behavior is at the root of a company's problems.

Another example: it takes extraordinary moral courage for a compensation consultant to tell a CEO that he is overpaid. In too many instances, conveyers of such news would soon find themselves out of a job. Even if one is not fired, the penalty for losing a major client in a professional services firm is a fate worse than death: derailment from the partnership track. As the demise of the Arthur Andersen accountancy demonstrated, the incentives in most professional firms too often encourage people to lie to, and for, clients. And that won't change unless the ways in which professionals are evaluated and rewarded change.

THE LEGACY OF ENRON

In the wake of Arthur Andersen, Enron, and similar instances of corporate lies and fraud uncovered over the last decade, increasing calls have been made in this country for transparency—that is, for business organizations free of dirty little secrets, the unveiling of which would destroy trust, ruin reputations, and wreak havoc with profits. In fact, there really is no need for *any* business secrets in organizations beyond protecting plans for new products and processes and other sources of competitive advantage (protecting the personal privacy of employees is a different matter). As my colleague Edward Lawler has shown, it even redounds to the benefit of organizations to post everyone's salary.[9]

The centrality of transparency to organizational health is well documented. In a hundred studies, the University of Denver's Carl Larsen found that "openness" is the primary predictor of success in work teams.[10] Transparency turns out to be in the long-term interest of all organizations. Indeed, it most often is in the *self*-interest of the very leaders who, paradoxically, refuse to listen to those who would bring them useful information. In this regard, one clear-headed manager is reported to have said, "The only messenger that I would ever shoot is one who arrived too late." Alarmingly, facts show that most employees will not even attempt to deliver an unpleasant message. In a recent scientific survey of a cross-section of American workers, over two-thirds report having personally witnessed unethical behavior on the job, but only about a third of those say they reported what they observed to their supervisors. The reasons given for their reticence range from fear of retaliation to the belief that management would not act on the information appropriately.[11] The missing element, in essence, is *trust*. Employees will not speak truth to power because they mistrust how those above them will respond. This is a disturbing conclusion, because, if there is one clear moral lesson about organizations, it is that trust is an essential ingredient to their effectiveness. The problem is that most leaders do not know how to create a bond of trust with followers.

FRAGILE TRUST

Shortly after the terrorist attack on the World Trade Center, I received a call from a CEO asking advice about how he should act in a time of crisis. I knew him well enough to understand what he was really asking: "What can I say that my people will believe?" Unfortunately, I couldn't offer any useful advice, because the leadership "secret ingredient" he was looking for—trust—cannot be created quickly. In fact, trust is the most elusive and fragile aspect of leadership.

Trust, along with shared cultural assumptions, is the strongest glue binding people together in groups. Whenever followers are asked to rank what they require of leaders, trust is always at the top of the list. But leaders can't provide trust directly to followers. Instead, trust is an *outcome* of all a leader's accumulated actions and behaviors. When leaders are candid, open, consistent, and predictable in their dealings with followers, the result will almost always be a condition of trust. Leaders who always tell the truth will perforce tell everyone the same thing; they will not be continually changing their story. The resulting constancy allows followers to act with the assurance that the rules of the game won't suddenly change, and that they will not be treated arbitrarily. Given that assurance, followers become more willing to stick their necks out, make an extra effort, put themselves on the line to help leaders achieve goals, and tell the truth themselves.

Such constancy is difficult for many leaders to maintain because it requires the relatively rare trait of integrity. People with integrity mean what they say and practice what they preach. This requires more than knowing what they believe; it is also necessary that they know themselves. Integrity comes naturally to leaders who, like Gandhi, know themselves and never have to wonder, "Now, just what do I believe in?" That's why Gandhi never had to remind himself what he had last said to this or that person, and why he could speak confidently without reference to a text or to notes. As the old saying goes, "When you tell the truth, you never have to *remember* what you said."

In practice, then, trust is created by the behavior of leaders toward followers: When leaders treat followers with respect, followers respond with trust. Leaders show their respect by always treating followers as ends in themselves—and never as means to achieve their own ego or power needs, or even to achieve the legitimate goals of the organization. Leaders demonstrate their respect by giving followers relevant information, by never using or manipulating them, and by including them in the making of decisions that affect them. Of course, leaders often say that it is impossible to practice such inclusion all the time; be that as it may, showing respect for people by including them in the flow of relevant information is the essence of transparency and trust. As one CEO explained, "In the absence of trust, all ambiguous behavior is viewed with suspicion . . . and, by definition, all behavior is ambiguous!" That's why the failure to include people is the second-most-common source of mistrust, close behind the failure of leaders to tell the truth consistently.

Unfortunately, the prevailing leadership ideology—called contingency theory—unwittingly leads to the creation of mistrust because it encourages managers to shift course arbitrarily and to do whatever they think expedient to achieve their goals, including going back on their word. To renege on one's word may seem necessary to some leaders, but in the eyes of followers it is a betrayal of trust. So when I received the 9/11 distress call from the CEO asking for help, I understood the predicament he was in. Even though his intentions were good, he feared that his actions in the light of the tragedy would be mistrusted by followers. In all probability, his fear was well founded, for trust must be earned over time through the accretion of positive acts and cannot be created with the wave of the executive hand in a time of crisis. In essence, trust is hard to earn, easy to lose, and, once lost, nearly impossible to regain.

Creating trust has practical implications affecting the willingness of followers to speak truth to power. When social psychologists Robert Blake and Jane Mouton examined data from a 1970s NASA study designed to uncover the human factors involved in airline accidents, they discovered that the habitual ways in which pilots interacted with their crews determined whether or not crewmembers would provide essential information to the pilots in the midst of an in-air crisis. Intact cockpit crews—pilot, copilot, navigator—were placed in flight simulators and tested to see how they would respond within the crucial thirty to forty-five seconds between the first sign of a potential accident and the fatal moment when it could no longer be averted. The researchers found that the stereotypical take-charge flyboy pilots who acted immediately on their gut instincts were far more likely to make the wrong decisions in trying to avoid disaster than were the more open and inclusive pilots who said to their crews, "We've got a problem. How do you read it?" before they made up their minds on a course of corrective action.

This finding probably shouldn't come as a surprise. After all, there is the old saw that "none of us is as smart as all of us," and at another level the lesson of the study is simple: leaders are far more likely to make mistakes when they act on too little information than when they wait to learn more.

But Blake and Mouton went deeper in their analysis, demonstrating that the pilots who made the right choices had habitually engaged in open exchanges with their crews, while crewmembers who had worked regularly with the "decisive" pilots were unwilling to intervene with their take-charge bosses—even when they had information that might well have saved the plane. In effect, the latter crewmembers thought to themselves, "Who am I to challenge his authority?" Blake and Mouton go on to make the obvious analogy: "Such attitudes create real problems for management, from top to bottom, whether the manager is the captain of a 747 with 400 passengers on board, the manager of a crew of forest fire fighters, the executive in the boardroom, or the supervisor on the shop floor."[12]

In essence, the silent crew members knew from experience that their leaders were not going to listen to them, wouldn't listen even if they volunteered useful information, and worse, were likely to reprimand them if they dared "speak out of turn." It's a matter of trust. And it is the leaders themselves and their organizations who suffer most in untrusting cultures. By not listening to what they don't want to hear, too many leaders shut out sources of potentially useful information.

Transparency, trust, and speaking truth to power are complexly interrelated ethical and organizational concepts. To create cultures that manifest those characteristics, leaders must do several practical things: provide equal access to information to all, refrain from punishing those who constructively demonstrate imperial nakedness, refrain from rewarding spurious loyalty, and empower and reward principled contrarians. But that is easier said than done, as recent experiences at the highest levels of government illustrate.

A HIGHLY
VISIBLE LESSON

As much as an unimpeded flow of information is the sine qua non of a business organization's ability to meet competitive challenges, the free flow of information is also a necessity for a democracy to flourish. A dozen or so books written by Washington insiders published over the last few years document the costs in terms of careers, reputations, and even lives when America's political leaders have been unwilling to listen to uncomfortable truths. Just before the start of the Iraq War in 2003, General Eric Shinseki told Congress that many more troops than had been planned for would be needed to stabilize that country after the U.S. invasion. Soon after his testimony, Shinseki's role was marginalized by the administration: Secretary of Defense Donald Rumsfeld rebuked him, and the deputy secretary, Paul Wolfowitz, claimed that the general's troop estimate was "wildly off the mark." Shinseki soon retired, but the lesson to other generals was clear, as Kori Schake, former director of defense strategy on the National Security Council, explained: "It served to silence critics just at the point in time when, internal to the process, you most wanted critical judgment."[13] At about the same time, Pentagon estimates of the potential cost of the war were running around the $50 billion mark. When White House economic adviser Lawrence Lindsey predicted, more realistically, that the cost could run to $200 billion, he was fired by the president.

In *State of Denial*, Bob Woodward cites an exchange in the Oval Office concerning the occupation of Iraq that eerily echoes

DeLorean's hypothetical 1970s discussion at GM headquarters cited earlier. According to Woodward, Secretary of State Colin Powell tried to explain to President George W. Bush and National Security Advisor Condoleezza Rice that a major problem in Baghdad was that there were two chains of command, both reporting to Secretary of Defense Donald Rumsfeld:

> The president looked surprised.
>
> "That's not right," Rice said. "That's not right."
>
> Powell thought Rice could at times be pretty sure of herself, but he was pretty sure he was right.
>
> "Yes, it is," Powell insisted.
>
> "Wait a minute," Bush interrupted, taking Rice's side. "That doesn't sound right."[14]

In *The One Percent Doctrine,* Ron Suskind describes how the president met foreign policy challenges with "self-generated certainty":

> The policy process, in fact, never changed much. Issues argued, often vociferously, at the level of deputies and principals rarely seemed to go upstream in their fullest form to the President's desk; and, if they did, it was often after Bush seemed to have already made up his mind based on what was so often cited as his "instinct" or "gut."[15]

And, in *The Price of Loyalty*, Suskind documents how former Treasury Secretary Paul O'Neil also faced such presidential certainty with regard to economic policy. O'Neil says that he would present a detailed policy argument to the president, who would respond with a blank stare, saying nothing, and then moving on to the next subject: "I wondered, from the first, if the President didn't know the questions to ask," O'Neil recalled, "or did he know and just not want to know the answers?"[16] In this and similar instances documented by other observers, instead of asking questions to gather information, the president kept his own counsel and made up his own mind.

Significantly, such criticisms of the way decisions are made in the Bush administration come, for the most part, from former White House insiders and nonpartisan sources. For example, *New York Times* columnist David Brooks proffers this advice on "how the next president needs to fix decision-making":

> The next president has to restore cabinet government—set up teams of rivals, as Lincoln, Eisenhower and Reagan did. . . . A president who vests power in cabinet members gives himself colleagues, people of similar age and stature who can argue with him face to face. By formalizing a decision-making process he balances egotistical secretaries against each other. A Rumsfeld would have to go to meetings and explain himself to his rivals. Entire departments couldn't be shut out of the loop, the way Treasury and State were.[17]

Clearly, it is not desirable to have an indecisive, Hamlet-like president. All presidents need sufficient self-confidence to make tough decisions. But the very strengths of leaders are often also their weaknesses. In this regard, Warren Bennis calls attention to the importance of what he calls "the Wallenda Factor," that supreme self-confidence found among most great leaders, a belief not only that they are right, but that they cannot fail.[18] When the leader is, in fact, right—as Churchill was right in the 1930s about the threat posed by the Nazis and hence refused to heed the counsel of the many appeasers in his country— such resolve and determination become the stuff of legend. But when a leader is wrong, or when conditions change, the very same trait appears as self-defeating stubbornness (witness Creon).

Because we know from experience that indecisive leaders are ineffective, we are all too prone to rush to the conclusion that the man or woman "in charge" should behave with certainty. In fact, it is the trait of *confidence,* and not certainty, that is required in a leader. Confident leaders are able to own up to their own mistakes and thus make effective midcourse corrections. In this regard, Francis Bacon offered leaders sound advice some four hundred years ago: "If a man will begin with certainties, he will end in doubts; but if he will be content to begin in doubts, he will end in certainties."

Perhaps the main reason why so many leaders stubbornly refuse to listen to subordinates is that they fear the news they carry is of the boss's own mistakes. Nobody likes to admit he is wrong but, as Lao Tsu wrote six hundred years before the birth of Christ, in the long run it is self-defeating for a leader not to do so:

> A great nation is like a great man:
>
> When he makes a mistake, he realizes it.
>
> Having realized it, he admits it.
>
> Having admitted it, he corrects it.
>
> He considers those who point out his faults
>
> As his most benevolent teachers.
>
> He thinks of his enemy as the shadow that he himself casts.

The problems attendant to speaking truth to power have been around forever, and are hence unlikely to magically vanish in the future. Nevertheless, experience shows that several things can be done to ameliorate these problems, and that both leaders and followers have moral obligations with regard to these actions.

RESPONSIBILITIES OF MESSENGERS

When one reports to an emperor, the temptation is to avoid bearing bad news. Worse, organizations have built-in rewards for flatterers and for those who appeal to the vanity of the leader. Here ego is to blame, not only on the part of the listener but on the part of the messenger, as well. In Arthur Schlesinger Jr.'s recently published diaries, he notes that during the Vietnam War key members of President Lyndon Johnson's cabinet had looked to Ambassador at Large W. Averell Harriman to convey their conviction that the war could not be won and that the sensible course was "withdrawal with honor." But Harriman remained silent because, as Schlesinger noted to a friend at the time, "Everyone has his weaknesses, and Averell's is the desire to be near power."[19] More recently, CIA Director George Tenet, who had a reputation as an honest, competent, and hard-working civil servant in the Clinton administration, nonetheless had his ego wounded during that period because he was never accepted as a White House insider. Later, as the only high-level Clinton-era holdover in the Bush administration, Tenet was understandably flattered when the new president's inner circle treated him as an integral member of their team. It is easy to see how Tenet would not want to jeopardize his newly won status by being the skunk at the party. Doubtless, nothing could cement his standing with the new team more than telling them what they wanted to hear with regard to Iraq and weapons of mass destruction.

In sharp distinction, during World War II, General George Marshall was noted for his backbone in standing up to the often bullying President Franklin D. Roosevelt. Historian Michael Beschloss notes an instance when Roosevelt tried to pressure Marshall to delay the development of ground forces. As everyone else in the room bowed to their boss's will, Marshall stood firm: "I am sorry Mr. President but I don't agree with that at all." Later, Marshall again stood up to the iron-willed president and offered his independent reading of the war effort, ultimately convincing his boss to commit to war funding during a tight presidential campaign, even though Roosevelt thought it would "send the wrong signal." Beschloss concludes, "Had Marshall kept quiet to please the boss, the United States Army would not have been so well prepared when the Japanese attacked Pearl Harbor."[20]

It is not easy to know when to speak out and when to hold one's tongue. Treasury Secretary Paul O'Neil, in contrast to George Tenet, made it a habit to speak truth to power and, ultimately, was fired by the administration because he was not seen as a "team player." The moral challenge O'Neil faced almost daily during his tenure in Washington was to weigh the balance between two competing goods: the frequently opposed organizational virtues of loyalty, on one hand, and truth telling, on the other. The character trait needed to appropriately adjust that balance is one to which I have already referred: *integrity*. In Stephen Carter's book on the subject, the distinguished Yale law professor lays out three requisite steps for the exercise of integrity:

1. *Discerning* what is right and what is wrong

2. *Acting* on what you have discerned, even at personal cost

3. *Saying openly* that you are acting on your understanding of right and wrong

The first step captures the idea of integrity as requiring a degree of moral reflectiveness. The second brings in the ideal of an integral person as steadfast, which includes the sense of keeping commitments. The third reminds us that a person of integrity is unashamed of doing the right thing.[21]

However, Carter stresses that the exercise of integrity is not as simple as one, two, three. Indeed, integrity, by and of itself, is an insufficient virtue: after all, radical ideologues can have oodles of it. Yet, at the same time, all other virtues are insufficient without integrity. President Richard Nixon had vision, intelligence, and courage, but those virtues proved not to be enough without the catalyst of integrity. Moreover, integrity does not simply entail telling the truth. Carter calls attention to "the insufficiency of honesty," reminding us that we also have other—often competing—responsibilities. As every family knows, inappropriate or careless truth telling can be hurtful, and ultimately fatal, to relationships.

In fact, great unintentional harm can be done when speaking truthfully. That's why managers find it so difficult to give candid performance appraisals to subordinates whose work is not up to par. Because giving negative feedback is nearly as unpleasant as firing people, most managers shy away from giving such appraisals even though they realize that an honest assessment of underperformance is in the interest of their organization and also of the subordinate receiving the bad news. And since offering negative feedback upward—to one's boss—is even more unpleasant, that occurs in organizations more rarely still. While there is no way to make giving feedback fun for the bearers of negative assessments and for the recipients above or below them, Frank Daly (the recently retired "dean" of corporate ethics officers) teaches that it is advisable for people in organizations to "practice having unpleasant conversations." Since there are both constructive and harmful ways to do so, it behooves speakers of truth to learn how to engage in the former—and to avoid the latter.

In sum, before speaking truth to power can be considered virtuous, the act must meet several criteria:

- It must be truthful.

- It must do no harm to innocents.

- It must not be self-interested (the benefits must go to others, or to the organization).

- It must be the product of moral reflection.

- It must come from a messenger who is willing to pay the price.

- It must have at least a chance of bringing about positive change (there is no virtue in tilting at windmills).

- It must not be done out of spite or anger.

This list is neither complete nor all-inclusive, and meeting each criterion requires considerable ethical analysis, as I explore in the following sections.

MORALLY COURAGEOUS— OR JUST CRAZY WITH ANGER?

In his *Nicomachean Ethics*, Aristotle offered a few practical tests for whether one's desire to speak truth to power was virtuous or merely driven by spite (as Daniel Goleman and I have each noted elsewhere).[22] He called attention to this matter because, throughout recorded history, the two main defenses used against organizational dissidents have been first to challenge their loyalty, and second to dismiss them as angry, perhaps insane, malcontents. In 2006, former White House pollster Matthew Dowd publicly expressed remorse for his hand in having promoted the Iraq war. As *New York Times* columnist Frank Rich reported, Dowd was "promptly patronized as an incipient basket case by an administration flack who attributed Mr. Dowd's defection to 'personal turmoil.'"[23] Two years earlier, the administration had argued that criticisms leveled against it by counterterrorism expert Richard Clarke should be discounted because the ex-White House aide's judgment was warped by anger. That argument gained some traction with the public: understandably, Americans expect a level of institutional loyalty from public servants, and find unseemly those who kiss and tell (especially those "jilted" by their bosses and who, thus, are trying to "even the score"). And it did appear Clarke had become seriously disgruntled when he found himself out of the loop at the White House and his input ignored by National Security Advisor Rice.[24] But how would one know if Clarke's undeniable anger was justified, on one hand, or so emotionally inflamed as to discredit the veracity of his critique, on the other?

This becomes a practical question that many employees— for example, those considering whistle-blowing—need to ask about themselves before they act. Indeed, the most gut-wrenching moments almost all of us experience on the job come when we have to choose between speaking up and remaining silent when we believe our bosses are making serious errors in judgment. Since no one wants to be seen as striking out wildly in anger, before we act we need to know if our own motives are virtuous, and if our response is appropriate. But how do we know? Aristotle says it takes time and effort to build the habits of ethical analysis that will allow us to know how to respond appropriately in morally-charged situations. For example, he says everyone gets angry from time to time, but he praises the person who is prone to go red-faced with anger *but has learned to control it*. In general, he concludes, it is virtuous to be able to remain even-tempered. But he doesn't stop there. He goes on to say there are times when anger is called for and appropriate. In fact, if one does not become angry over a grave injustice, he says, one cannot be considered virtuous. The secret lies in knowing when to be angry—and then how to direct that emotion usefully. The virtuous person, Aristotle says, becomes angry *at the right time, over the right issue, and to the right degree*. He then cites examples of questions we might ask of ourselves to develop the moral muscles needed to allow us to meet those three criteria habitually:

- When is my anger a direct response to a clear moral wrong?
- Where is the most useful place to draw the line and pick a fight?
- When is my anger justified by the offense?
- To what degree is my response commensurate with the level of the offense?

ORGANIZATIONAL EXAMPLES

A quick review of what social scientists have to say about the behavior of indignant employees in public and private organizations provides a modern framework for understanding Aristotle's ancient ethical perspective. In the early 1970s, the economist Albert O. Hirschman posited that employees who disagree with company policy have only three options: "exit, voice, and loyalty."[25] That is, they can offer a principled resignation, or try to change the policy (speak truth to power), or remain loyal team players despite their opposition. Experience shows that most people choose option three, the path of least resistance. They swallow whatever moral objections they may have to questionable dictates from above, concluding they lack power to change things or, worse, will be punished if they attempt to do so. Indeed, such loyalty is assumed: most executives expect employees will be "good soldiers" and not question company policy (or, if they do, will go away quietly).

But sometimes employees find the actions of their bosses so unconscionable that they feel they have no choice but to resign and go public. Typically, this is the last resort for those who have voiced disagreement internally and exhausted all channels of appeal but still feel they were not given a serious hearing. On rare occasions, a respected and powerful organizational insider will proffer such a principled resignation but, typically, those who quit over matters of principle are powerless people who have been pushed to the extreme of quitting by the disrespect shown to them by superiors. After all, how many employees would resign if they felt they had been listened to, and their opinions respected—even if they didn't get their way on a matter of principle? In general, people have to be angry as hell before they quit and go public. And, because anger is such an unattractive, unsettling, and even frightening trait, angry people seldom have much influence, and they are easily dismissed by those in power as out of control, or "in turmoil."

But anger can be a socially useful fuel, as the wrathful 2004 presidential candidacy of Howard Dean illustrates. Dean seemed legitimately angry over the administration's decision to invade a country that he believed had no intention of attacking America and presented no real threat to the nation's security. His anger-fueled campaign served the purpose of mobilizing his party to challenge the administration's war policies (those Democrats who weren't "angry enough" had acquiesced to the invasion of Iraq). Even though he was a member of the opposition party whose supposed duty is to offer loyal criticism, Dean paid a price: his hostile demeanor was ridiculed by allies and foes alike (late-night talk show hosts David Letterman and Jay Leno feasted on Dean for months). And, when Dean ultimately went red-faced wiggy on national television after a primary loss, he obviously blew it by Aristotle's standards of appropriate anger: he got angry at the wrong place, to the wrong degree, and over the wrong issue.

In contrast to such highly visible politicians, angry ex-employees risk a lot more than being mocked by television hosts: they open themselves to attacks on their personal lives by the considerable force of their threatened institutions. That's why most workers have to be totally teed off before they violate the norms of organizational loyalty. To get angry enough to face an onslaught on one's character and veracity requires not only fundamental disagreement over policy—typically involving the conviction that a moral principle has been violated—but also deep personal hurt. Such were the mixed motivations in recent high-profile corporate cases of whistle-blowing at cigarette-maker Brown and Williamson and at Unum Provident Insurance. In both instances, corporate leaders responded with the standard organizational defense that the whistleblowers' testimony should be discounted because they were "disgruntled" (the ex-employees were portrayed as angry "nut cases" with enough skeletons in their closets to outfit a Halloween ball).

If dissidents aren't called crazy, they are portrayed as disloyal—and treason, after all, is a capital offense. The charge of disloyalty is as easy for leaders to bring against followers as it is difficult for the accused to counter and disprove. Moreover, since loyalty is typically an admirable trait, it is also a convenient blind for cowardly followers to hide behind. In early 2007, a long-term, high-ranking French *fonctionnaire* named Maurice Papon died at age ninety-six. He had served loyally under, sequentially, the last French government prior to the outbreak of World War II, the Nazi-collaborating Vichy government during the war, and General de Gaulle's postwar government. In all three administrations he was known for his competence, efficiency, and commitment to his work—even when his job under the Nazis entailed shipping French Jews off to Auschwitz to face certain death, or killing up to two hundred Algerians and disposing of their bodies in the Seine under de Gaulle. As *The Economist* noted in its obituary of Papon, he was ever-loyal to a code of silence about the misdeeds of whomever he worked for, and lived committed to "a duty to survive, to keep things running, to avoid gratuitous provocation that might make a bad case worse."[26] He was, of course, rewarded for his loyalty by those above him, much as cowardly American corporate and government organizational functionaries are today rewarded by those they serve.

Recently, General Ricardo Sanchez responded to charges that the top brass of the U.S. military had been unwilling to stand up and tell the truth to the administration and the public with regard to the situation in Iraq: "The worst thing is to have officers question high-ranking political officials." This is a commonly held view, not just in the military but in business organizations as well. But is questioning authority really the *worst thing*—worse, say, than the needless deaths of thousands of soldiers and civilians? In the private sector, is it really worse for managers to challenge top executives than it is to stand by "loyally" while the company loses profits or its reputation?

Many institutional leaders believe that their employees owe loyalty to *them* as individuals. In contrast, whistleblowers typically say they owe their first allegiance to their organizations. Indeed, it is when employees believe their leaders betray their organization's integrity that their anger mounts sufficiently to justify the risks of whistle-blowing. Nothing makes formerly loyal employees angrier than values-betraying leaders who claim *"L'etat, c'est moi."* In this context, Aristotle reminds us that the overall good of the state (the group or organization) takes moral precedence over the personal needs of its leaders.

Hence, to the Bush administration's charge that such critics as former Treasury Secretary Paul O'Neil, Ambassador Joseph Wilson, pollster Matthew Dowd, and national security expert Richard Clarke were "disloyal" and "too angry" to be trusted, Aristotle would say, "Those who are not angry at the things they should be angry at are thought to be fools." Indeed, if they weren't angry they would still be inside, loyally carrying out orders, or trying to voice disagreement through established processes. But these men had tried that, failed in their attempts to be heard, and then opted for vocal exits. Doubtless, it would be prettier if whistleblowers weren't so angry, but anger is often a necessary spur to doing the right thing. Indeed, what might have happened had Secretary of State Colin Powell allowed his reported anger over the decision to invade Iraq to overcome his military-disciplined instinct to loyally fall into line with administration policies? Had he instead resigned and publicly voiced his concerns, would Americans then have been so accepting of the questionable evidence on weapons of mass destruction? Who knows? But it does seem clear that if we too quickly ignore the angry words of disgruntled former officials, fewer of them will be willing to step forward, and there will be fewer safeguards of the public interest. Aristotle adds one important admonition: "The good-tempered man is not revengeful."

A PERSONAL EXAMPLE

In hindsight, I wish I had applied Aristotle's and Hirschman's ethical tests before I made what was doubtless the worst public error of my life: I simply quit when the leaders of the organization I worked for betrayed its essential values. Because I had firmly believed in those values, my response was over-the-top emotional: I became mad as hell. When I expressed that anger to colleagues and friends, their response was "Cool it. They're not going to change, so it won't do you any good to get angry. If you can't live with the situation, then just quit. But don't burn bridges by making a stink." One friend went so far as to tell me that my anger was "unattractive." Frankly, I didn't know what to do. I didn't know how to think about the issue, and didn't know how to behave. But since the only thing more damning that can be said about an employee than he is "angry" is that he is "disloyal," I bottled up my emotions, quit, and went quietly away.

Years later, when the organization had completely abandoned its founding principles and purpose, I found myself still angry and not at all certain that I had done the right thing. In retrospect, I see that I had not applied basic tests of ethical analysis before I acted precipitously. I had not considered all my options. I had not considered all the consequences of my action. I had not considered the needs and capabilities of all the organization's stakeholders. In short, I acted out of anger and not as the result of moral reflection. Applying Aristotle's tests, I now feel my response was, at best, half right. Clearly, I was right to be incensed when the people I reported to put their own self-interest above the good of the organization. But I don't think I channeled my anger in a useful way. Before I quit, I should have tried to offer them a constructive path by which they could have gotten back on track. And I now think I erred in not having the moral courage to "go public" to call attention to what was happening. Had I reached out to powerful outsiders—such as members of the organization's board—who also cared about its founding values, I might have prevented the leaders from damaging its integrity. For that course to have succeeded, I would have had to be clearly acting for the good of the organization, and not in a "revengeful" spirit.

Aristotle's insight that virtuous people become angry at the right time, over the right issue, and to the right degree allows me now to see that my act of quitting had no constructive impact. Had I asked myself the ethical questions Aristotle raises, I think I might have directed my anger more positively and gotten rid of it much sooner. Indeed, I even might have effectively spoken truth to power.

Those complications duly registered, it can be said that we all have a moral obligation to speak truth to power when the actions of leaders are harmful to our organization, to people inside and outside the organization, and to the leaders themselves. But as hard as it is for messengers to fulfill such obligations, it is far more difficult for leaders to listen to, and heed, the warnings of followers.

RESPONSIBILITIES OF LISTENERS

In response to the Enron scandal, a mini industry of compliance consultants has been created. These firms offer systems and programs designed to root out bad apples down organizational ranks. There is more than a little "blaming the victim" involved in these efforts because, in fact, creating a culture of candor starts with the behavior of those at the top of the organization. Leaders who tell the truth, admit mistakes, and respectfully listen to the perspectives of others set the tone for an entire culture. This is simple, obvious, and clear as day. Yet, as the current leaders of both political parties in Washington illustrate, these positive behaviors are unnatural among those in positions of power. Indeed, most leaders in both the public and private sectors have to work to overcome culturally conditioned reflexes to dissemble, to deny, and to blame others.

In the late 1970s, ARCO president Thornton Bradshaw would meet regularly with his company's managers to discuss how to respond to inquiries from the press. His first rule: *always tell the truth*. Bradshaw assured his managers that they never would be second-guessed by the company if they simply told what they knew when asked. Long before the Watergate scandal hammered the point home, he argued that the most unforgivable sins are lying and covering up. Bradshaw's second rule: *admit it when you are wrong*. He argued, as a general proposition, that no one ever stayed in hot water if they candidly and contritely admitted they had erred. And Bradshaw was not only the first top executive in a major corporation to meet regularly with his employees, the press, shareholders, and regulators in open exchanges, he also frequently interacted with his industry's critics in the labor, environmental, and product safety movements, listening with respect to their various perspectives. On Bradshaw's watch, ARCO never experienced even a minor ethical or legal scandal, a record that was rare for an oil company in that era.

Recently, the *Wall Street Journal* reported on the leadership behavior of a contemporary executive who, apparently, behaves much in the way Bradshaw did thirty years ago. Kent Thiry, CEO of DaVita, a dialysis-treatment operator, meets with his employees regularly asking them for candid feedback so that he—and the company—can avoid "messing up." When employees told him everything was going hunky-dory in the process of absorbing a recent acquisition, he shook off their good news and replied, "Either you are all on drugs, or better than me, because integrations are a god-awful nightmare." Thiry actually seeks out bad news and rewards those who give it to him. In an industry that is a sitting target for consumer lawsuits, he resolutely collects data from all sources—customers, suppliers, employees, even ex-employees—trying to identify the practices that, if left unchecked, could come back to haunt him and the organization. His top management team then systematically acts to correct aspects of the business that employees say need fixing. It would seem that Thiry's entire approach to leadership is predicated on speaking truth to power.[27] What leaders need to learn from such examples is that it is not enough simply to have an "open door policy," an organizational ombudsman, or protection for whistleblowers—although all those things are useful. What matters most is to have that culture of candor starting right at the top of the company.

Unfortunately, too few corporate leaders today behave like Bradshaw and Thiry, and too many are unwilling to open their ears to things they would rather not hear. Too many are like Enron's Kenneth Lay, whose leadership behavior was reminiscent of that macho odd couple Mao Zedong and Douglas MacArthur, of whom David Halberstam wrote: "Neither of their staffs ever told them a thing they didn't want to hear."[28] As the ancient example of Creon reminds us, it is often the presence of excessive amounts of testosterone that leads to a loss of hearing. It is almost always ego—and almost always ego of the male persuasion—that makes it futile, even dangerous, to speak truth to power. As Bennis, Goleman, and Biederman detail in Essay One, leaders would do well to reflect on their own receptivity to suggestions, alternative points of views, and others' opinions. "One motive for turning a deaf ear to what others have to say seems to be sheer hubris," they point out—a malady that often affects leaders who believe they are wiser or more expert than those they lead, and who tend to become unwilling to turn to others for advice.

That is why I believe the mantle of true greatness should be reserved for those leaders who possess the so-called feminine virtues of humility, inclusion, vulnerability, service to others, and respect for people. The behavior of the late President Gerald Ford serves as a positive reminder of what great leadership entails. Shortly after Ford died, Frank Rich noted that the former president "encouraged dissent in his inner circle. He had no enemies, no ego, no agenda, no ideology, no concern for his image."[29] A day earlier, on the same op-ed page of the *Times*, Harvard historian Orlando Patterson described attending a meeting at the White House in which Ford listened intently, and with humility, to the points made by a diverse group of experts, showing equal respect to those with whom he agreed and to those with whom he disagreed.

President Ford was unlike the macho political and business leaders whose faces typically occupy the front page of news and business magazines. And, as a business professor, I can attest that Ford's traits of leadership are not the ones advocated in most business schools today, where "take-charge decisiveness" is prized over the ability to listen. In short, Americans are getting the kind of leadership our society celebrates. That being the case, we cannot expect a sea change in the behavior of those who should be more open to candor without a change in the context in which leaders operate.

ORGANIZATIONAL RESPONSIBILITIES

In the private sector, constructive change will not occur until corporations consciously begin to select, train, develop, and reward leaders who listen—that is, Gerald Fords in the making. Yet, in an ongoing study of top managers in large corporations, my research colleagues and I have found that executives are far more often selected for their proven ability to compete with their fellow members in the executive suite than for their demonstrated teamwork. This selection system encourages the hoarding of information, which then frequently leads to conflict. Changing that system is the responsibility of boards of directors, the people who have the ultimate responsibility for choosing leaders. Truly independent boards also would go a long way toward providing a needed check on executive ego, and a source of objective, disinterested truth telling to often-deaf ears.

If anything is clear, it is that executives will not begin to act virtuously as long as boards continue to reward misbehavior. For example, Raytheon Corporation's board had claimed that promoting ethical behavior was a criterion it used in setting executive bonuses. Yet, shortly after the company's CEO admitted that he had plagiarized large parts of a book he had claimed to have written himself, the board voted him a $2.6 million bonus. When pressed, a spokesman for the board explained that they had plainly stated that ethics was "just one factor" they considered.[30] What counts in terms of creating a culture of candor, of course, is not what board members or executives say, it is what they do. When Jeffrey Skilling was CEO of Enron he was quoted as saying, "People have an obligation to dissent in this company. . . . If you don't speak up, that's not good." (At about the same time, Enron had distributed notepads containing the Martin Luther King quotation cited in the first paragraph of this essay.) So the first rule of management is that organizations get the behavior they reward—not the behavior they describe in their posted values statements.

Because denial, self-deception, and hypocrisy are such common features of organizational life, it is often useful for companies to bring in outside "anthropologists," independent observers skilled in identifying potentially toxic behaviors and the hidden values that drive them. In 1973, Warren Bennis and I coined the term "organizational culture" and created a diagnostic tool to identify the unique behavioral characteristics of a company—for example, profiling the type of person who tends to get ahead in an organization. One question we asked was, "What is the company joke that no one would dare to tell the boss?"[31] Since it is the values of leaders that drive organizational behavior, any process that serves to surface those will help in establishing a climate of candor. When managers honestly and objectively start to ask, "What do we *really* cherish and hold dear—quality? technical excellence? power? executive privilege?"—organizations take a useful first step in that process.

Finally, actions that break down the artificial barriers that separate the few at the top of an organization from the many down the line serve to encourage an increased flow of information. In this regard, the continued executive resistance to such "best practices" as employee involvement and other forms of participation in decision making and information sharing is nothing short of remarkable, if not disturbing.[32] There truly is no excuse for it: nothing has to be invented to create an effective culture of candor. For example, for the last twenty years every employee at SRC Holdings has had access to all financial and managerial information, and each is taught how to interpret and apply it. The net effect, in the words of the company's CFO, "is like having 700 internal auditors out there in every function of the company."[33]

That is the definition of transparency, of a company with no secrets, one in which every employee is empowered to speak the truth. SRC Holdings' culture was created by CEO Jack Stack, who decided to forgo the ego-satisfying pleasure of being "the boss" and instead adopt the roles of teacher and listener. To do so, he had to learn to trust his employees with the managerial and financial information typically hoarded by executives in most companies, as he had to trust them to act responsibly on the basis of that information. I conclude that Stack's un-Creon-like behavior is what the ancient Greeks had in mind when they referred to "virtuous leadership." Now, 2,500 years later, all leaders have the moral obligation to heed the same advice that Creon's son had the courage to place in his father's all-too-deaf ear:

> Then do not have one mind, and one alone
> that only your opinion can be right.
> Whoever thinks that he alone is wise,
> his eloquence, his mind, above the rest,
> come the unfolding, shows his emptiness.
> A man, though wise, should never be ashamed
> of learning more, and must unbend his mind.
> Have you not seen the trees beside the torrent,
> the ones that bend them saving every leaf,

while the resistant perish root and branch?
And so the ship that will not slacken sail,
the sheet drawn tight, unyielding, overturns,
She ends the voyage with her keel on top.
No, yield your wrath, allow a change of stand.
Young as I am, if I may give advice,
I'd say it would be best if men were born
perfect in wisdom, but failing this
(which often fails) it can be no dishonor
to learn from others when they speak good sense.[34]

3

Warren Bennis

THE NEW TRANSPARENCY

The definition of *transparent* is simple enough. It means, in addition to the literal "capable of being seen through," "without guile or concealment; open; frank; candid." But in the last few years, *transparency* has acquired new implications. As a headline writer for *Fast Company* joked, "Transparency: It's Not Just for Shrink Wrap Anymore." Once largely reserved for international trade negotiations, it has surged in popularity. Now it seems that no American president, CEO, mayor, school official, or police chief can make a public pronouncement without using the word, usually with the implicit promise that his or her statement is true and motives pure. As a culture, we obviously long for our public institutions, our corporations, and our other organizations to be open and honest about their dealings. We want to be confident that our leaders are telling us the truth, the whole truth, and nothing but the truth in matters that involve our national security, the safety of the products we use, and the state of our economy. We want to believe that our government agencies are transparent and honorable, without secret prisons or secret agendas that reflect special interests rather than the public weal. We want to believe that, but we often do not. Despite the promise of transparency on so many lips, we often have the sinking feeling that we are not being told all that we need to know or have the right to know.

But at the same time, a countervailing force is making transparency less and less dependent on the will of those who run our institutions. The digital revolution has made transparency inevitable, not just in this country but worldwide. The Internet, camera-equipped cell phones, and the emergence over the last decade of the blogosphere have democratized power, shifting it inexorably away from the high-profile few to the technology-equipped many. Historians of the phenomenon say this new digital transparency was born barely a decade ago (in 1998) when online columnist Matt Drudge revealed that the *Washington Post* had quashed a story about then President Bill Clinton's dalliance with a White House intern.[1] Blogs began to multiply with the launch in 1999 of San Francisco–based blogger.com, a free site that helped users create their own online forums. Since then millions of blogs have sprung up around the world, and their collective clout has transformed politics, the mainstream media, indeed the public and private lives of people everywhere.

In the past, we often had to wait until a courageous whistle-blower came along before we learned an institution's secrets. Now a company's most incendiary internal memos may be disclosed by an anonymous blogger, without ties to any newspaper or television station but with inside knowledge, who can reach thousands, even millions of readers. The proliferation of networked computers has finally created the Global Village that Marshall McLuhan predicted more than a half-century ago. Now anyone with Internet access can take on the most powerful institutions on earth, without making any significant financial investment and often with little or no fear of reprisals.

The history of the U.S. Navy's swastika-shaped building complex illustrates how digital technology increasingly drives transparency.[2] In 1967 the Navy broke ground on a cluster of four L-shaped buildings on its Naval Base Coronado in San Diego. Not long afterward, someone pointed out that the buildings had the unfortunate characteristic of looking like a giant swastika when viewed from the air. Since the complex was in a civilian no-fly zone, Navy brass decided the best thing to do about the potential embarrassment was to keep quiet about it. Almost four decades later, however, some wired individual spotted the swastika-shaped complex among the satellite images available on Google Earth. In 2006 word of the inaptly shaped building leaped from the blogosphere to talk radio, then, in quick succession, to the leadership of the San Diego branch of the Anti-Defamation League, the city's Democratic Congresswoman Susan Davis, and *Los Angeles Times* reporter Tony Perry. At first, the Defense Department said it had no plans to change the complex. But in September 2007, the Navy announced it would spend more than $600,000 to obscure the complex's problematic shape with landscaping and modifications to its rooftops. As a spokeswoman for the base said, "We don't want to offend anyone, and we don't want to be associated with the [Nazi] symbol." And she explained, "You have to realize back in the 1960s we did not have the Internet."

GLOBAL TRANSPARENCY

To begin to understand how digital technology is creating greater transparency worldwide, it is useful to look first at the Opacity Index, launched in 2001. As its creator Joel Kurtzman explains in his 2007 book *Global Edge,* the index was developed in response to a question posed by former PriceWaterhouseCoopers CEO James Schiro, who wondered if a nation's transparency could be measured.[3] Kurtzman and his colleagues reasoned that opacity—the lack of transparency—could be measured even if transparency itself could not.

The resultant index gauges the economic cost to some fifty nations of their lack of transparency. Each country is evaluated in five areas of concern: corruption in business and government, ineffectiveness of its legal system, negative aspects of its economic policy, inadequacy of its accounting and governance practices, and detrimental aspects of its regulatory structures. The countries receive a numeric score in each area as well as an overall opacity rating. The higher the number, the less open the country. In the most recent index, in 2005, the United States was one of the five most transparent nations. Its overall opacity score of 21 trailed the United Kingdom, which had the best score of 14, Finland, and Hong Kong, and edged out Denmark, with an overall score of 22. At the other end of the transparency spectrum was Nigeria, which was the most opaque with a score of 60. Slightly more transparent were Lebanon, Indonesia, and Saudi Arabia, all with scores over 50. China's overall score was a fairly opaque 48.

Kurtzman and his colleagues argue that bribery, fraud, unenforceable contracts, and other opacity-related risks "represent the real costs to [global] business."[4] In their view, these frequent small-scale risks ultimately cause more economic harm than such rarer high-profile risks as natural disasters and terrorism. "These [opacity-related] risks interfere with commerce, add to costs, slow growth and make the future even more difficult to predict," the authors write. "They also deter investment." In the 2004 report, Matt Feshbach, chief investment officer of a Florida hedge fund, observes: "The key to any good investment relationship is clarity—the ability to see and even be in communication with what's really going on. It's the same whether it's a company, a country or a region."

It is useful to have a country's opacity score in mind when evaluating news about it, especially news relating to transparency. Consider China, for example. Despite its Communist government's continuing attempts to control the flow of information within China and between it and other nations, China is moving toward greater technology-driven openness. By 2008, China had 210 million Internet users and 47 million bloggers. And while the Chinese government diligently polices the Internet—limiting what people can access on Google, for instance—citizens are using the Internet to expose some of the most disturbing aspects of Chinese life.

Favoritism and bribing officials have long been scourges of life in China. In the 2005 Opacity Index China's corruption score was a considerable 65, high enough to put it among the ten most corrupt nations studied, along with Saudi Arabia, Indonesia, Pakistan, Russia, and, topping the list, Lebanon. But such time-honored Chinese practices as buying the silence of police are crumbling under the collective power of ordinary citizens with computer access. In June 2007, for example, the *Wall Street Journal* reported that parents went online to protest the kidnapping of children forced into slave labor in coal mines and brick factories in Henan and Shanxi provinces.[5] In part because of the parents' digital crusade, the government sent more than 45,000 police into the area, rescuing more than 500 people, and making more than 150 arrests. Before the parents took to their computers, some had tried to get local officials to find their children, some of them handicapped. But as one parent told the *Wall Street Journal,* "We contacted the local police, but they are protecting the brick-kiln owners. They wouldn't help us."

The rising power of China's new digerati hasn't turned every Chinese official into a champion of sunshine, any more than scrutiny from the blogosphere has loosed the lips of all American officials. The Chinese government still tries to keep a lid on its embarrassing secrets, including, recently, the number of citizens dying prematurely from pollution-related illnesses (more than 750,000 a year) and the outbreak of an Ebola-like disease in pigs. China's own mainstream media are kept on a tight leash, and foreign media are closely monitored. Besides digital pressure, other forces are making China more open, notably its desire to favorably impress the West at the 2008 Olympic Games in Beijing and an international expo in Shanghai in 2010. The West is also calling for greater transparency in the wake of lead-tainted toys, exploding tires, poison toothpaste, counterfeit diabetic testing strips, and other dangerous Chinese exports.

But the potential power of a billion Chinese citizens with Internet access and cell phone cameras cannot be ignored, even by a government that has a long history of holding information close. In April 2007, China issued new Regulations on Open Government Information that require the posting online of data about land use, public health investigations, and other official activities, starting May 1, 2008. For the first time, citizens will be able to request information from government agencies with the expectation of a response within fifteen days. Still off-limits to the public will be information that threatens "state security, public safety, normal economic operations, and social stability" as well as individuals' personal information, according to the *Wall Street Journal*.[6] In classic Chinese fashion, the content of the new regulations was kept secret until they were announced in April. But inside observers think the new rules represent a genuine shift in the direction of openness. As a media expert from the University of Hong Kong told the *Wall Street Journal* in March 2007, "This legislation is important in the sense that it changes presumptions about information in China, making release of information the rule rather than the exception."[7]

India is another vast nation where digital technology is boosting transparency. Deemed fairly corrupt by the Opacity Index (its corruption score was 57 in 2005), India is also undergoing profound technology-driven social change. In a 2004 article called "The Digital Village," *Business Week* reported on the impact computerization of more than 20 million land records has had on poor farmers in villages surrounding the high-tech capital of Bangalore.[8] In the past the farmers had access to their deeds only through village accountants who sometimes conspired with large landowners to cheat uneducated, lower-caste farmers out of their property. Now when small farmers need copies of their deeds to get bank loans for seed and other supplies, they can access the deeds at government-owned computer kiosks. The farmers can even print out the documents for 30 cents apiece, down from the $2 to $22 they paid to an accountant under the old system.

India has a relatively modest number of Internet users, an estimated 60 million in early 2008. But the government's high-tech kiosks are teaching the poor farmers an indelible lesson: digital technology changes the rules of the game and thus can transform their lives. Explains the Indian official who oversaw the computerization project: "With equal access to information, a lower-caste person now has the same privileges as an upper-caste person." That no doubt overstates the case. But the new transparency has given the villagers a new set of expectations. They dream of acquiring computers of their own and of sending their children off to study computer science, *Business Week* reports. In short, the villagers know that digital technology is the ladder that will let them climb out of the well to which poverty, social class, and tradition have consigned them.

The ability to access sympathetic Web sites and to blog is especially liberating in countries with repressive governments that can clamp down on newspapers and television stations far more readily than on the ethereal Internet. In such places, blogs can be tantamount to a digital resistance movement. A compelling posting on a blog can recruit thousands of readers to its point of view; each of those readers can send the message to thousands more, and soon the cry is heard around the world. Iran, for example, has an estimated 100,000 bloggers among its 5 million Internet users, including controversial blogger-in-chief President Mahmoud Ahmadinejad. Government pressure on Iranian bloggers varies from day to day. Once ignored by digitally illiterate religious authorities, bloggers now risk arrest. But pressure on them is less intense than it might be, given the country's fundamentalist climate, because "the government wants to look like a democracy," Iranian blogger Hossein Derakhshan told *Wired*'s Jeff Howe in June 2005.

Political blogs helped make the 2005 election "the most open and transparent . . . Iran has ever seen," according to *The Nation*. Before the election, in a piece called "Bloggers of Iran," the magazine speculated on how Iran's bloggers could reshape the Islamic republic: "While Iran remains a closed society, a fierce debate about the country's future is underway in the blogs. The coming election might not bring about much, if any, change in Iranians' lives, but the blogs could help open up that society, permitting the free flow of information and ideas like never before."[9]

Fear of transparency was the main reason for the digital crackdown on protesters by Myanmar's ruling military junta in the autumn of 2007. In contrast to past demonstrations, the anti-government protests that began in Myanmar in August were conducted in cyberspace as well as on the streets. When thousands of saffron-robed Buddhist monks gathered in the capital city of Yangon, they were surreptitiously photographed by video and cell phone cameras and the images distributed worldwide via the Internet. Sympathy for the protesters was fueled by such disturbing images as that of a Japanese photojournalist shot by government soldiers who continued taking pictures as he died in the street. Vividly documenting the cyber-revolt in the *New York Times,* Seth Mydans reports that protesters sent e-mail and instant messages, blogged, and posted updates on Facebook and Wikipedia.[10] For weeks, they evaded local authorities by sending reports electronically to online sympathizers in Thailand and elsewhere. In addition, Mydans writes, the dissidents "used Internet versions of 'pigeons'—the couriers that reporters used in the past to carry out film and reports—handing their material to embassies or non-government organizations with satellite connections."

But finally, Mydans writes, "the generals who run Myanmar simply switched off the Internet." That meant shutting down the country's two Internet providers. Just as the authorities seized cameras to stop the flow of images, they disrupted international telephone service to silence the protesters. The editor of a Thailand-based magazine for Burmese exiles recounted the last telephone call he got from one of his most reliable activist sources inside Myanmar: "We can no longer move around . . . we cannot do anything any more. We are down. We are hunted by soldiers—we are down."

At the time Mydans's piece was published, little news of dissent was trickling out of fear-filled Myanmar, a nation so opaque that outsiders who track transparency lack the data to evaluate it accurately. But Mydans quoted New York University professor Mitchell Stevens on the likelihood of the truth emerging eventually in the new era of the technology-empowered citizen journalist: "There are always ways people find of getting information out, and authorities always have to struggle with them. . . . There are fewer and fewer events that we don't have film images of; the world is filled with Zapruders" (alluding to Abraham Zapruder, the businessman who filmed John F. Kennedy's 1963 assassination).

THE ROLE OF BLOGS

Because of the blogosphere's ability to expose secrets to outsiders, George Washington University professor Michael Cornfield has described it as "half forensic lab and half tavern."[11] Web logs, as blogs are properly called, are also strange hybrids that combine multiple functions. Currently the most popular facilitator of Web logs, Google gave the trademarked name Blogger to the free application that allows users to set up their own sites. Google explains at Blogger.com: "A blog is a personal diary. A daily pulpit. A collaborative space. A political soapbox. A breaking-news outlet. A collection of links. Your own private thoughts. Memos to the world."

A blog is, in short, a tool. And as Steward Brand, one of the counterculture creators of the wired world, understood when he chose the phrase as the subtitle of his *Last Whole Earth Catalogue,* those who have "access to tools" have access to power. One notable denizen of the blogosphere is the corporate blogger. A handful of top executives have made names for themselves as bloggers, including General Motors' vice president and car guru Robert Lutz, who describes himself as "at the wheel of Fast-Lane blog." But the most effective corporate bloggers are often nonmanagers who allow outsiders to peek inside their companies and project a David-unafraid-of-the-corporate-Goliath persona despite collecting a paycheck. *Fortune* magazine featured a popular employee blogger from Microsoft, Robert Scoble, in a story on the pervasiveness of blogs.[12] Scoble's most notable achievement appears to be lessening the hostility routinely directed at his employer, so often treated as the Great Satan by the digital elite. Chairman Bill Gates told *Fortune* that Scoble's and other blogs by Microsoft staff have enhanced the company's image: "It's all about openness," Gates said. "People see them as a reflection of an open, communicative culture that isn't afraid to be self-critical."

By their nature, blogs challenge hierarchies, introducing an outsider's or non-elitist voice into the conversation at hand. When those voices are wise or even simply contrarian, they benefit the organization by challenging its dominant assumptions, preventing tunnel vision, and reminding the powers that be that they don't have a lock on all useful truths. Because the technology behind blogs includes creation of an index, the opinions and information they contain are relatively easy to access—a real plus in a world in which we are always at risk of being swamped by a tsunami of undifferentiated data.

Network pioneer John Patrick, former longtime vice president of Internet technology at IBM, offered a compelling vision of how blogs can aid companies and other organizations when he talked to *CIO Insight*'s Marcia Stepanek in 2003: "It's a way to energize the expertise from the bottom—in other words, to allow people who want to share, who are good at sharing, who know who the experts are, who talk to the experts or who may, in fact, be one of the experts, to participate more fully. We all know somebody in our organization who knows everything that's going on. 'Just ask Sally. She'll know.' There's always a Sally, and those are the people who become bloggers."[13]

THE WINNING CIRCLE

Energizing *all* the talent in an organization, not just that at the top or that of the chosen, increases productivity and value, and not just value resulting from better morale because of greater inclusiveness—no small thing in itself. I learned this firsthand more than sixty years ago when I was a graduate student at Massachusetts Institute of Technology. A group of social psychologists at MIT (I was among the most junior) conducted an elegant experiment that demonstrated that collaboration leads to better outcomes when solving complex problems—as virtually all our problems, beyond which tie to wear, are today. For the experiment, five subjects sat at a round table, hidden from each other by partitions.[14] Each subject received a box that contained six colored marbles. The participants were asked to choose the single one of their six marbles that was the same color as just one of each of the others' marbles. The subjects couldn't talk to each other, but they could share information by passing messages on index cards through slots in the partitions.

With the round table, we were able to simulate the flow of information in three kinds of organizations. We simulated the pyramidal bureaucracy that still persists in many organizations with what we called the Wheel. In that arrangement, all the messages went to a single person, the unseen leader. The Circle was the most collegial configuration. In it, each subject could pass messages to both immediate neighbors. We also had a configuration we called the Chain in which all the index cards were passed in one direction.

As soon as a subject felt sure which marble matched one of all the other subjects' marbles, that marble was dropped down a rubber tube in the table. The experimenter at the other end of the tube was able to measure the speed and accuracy with which the subjects chose their matching marbles. When the data were subsequently analyzed, the result was a landmark finding—solid empirical evidence that collaboration beats top-down control in complex decision making.[15]

I say *complex decision making* because when the task was easy—that is, when the marbles were all readily identified bright, single colors (called "puries" by aficionados)—the top-down Wheel was the most efficient configuration. But as soon as the task was made more difficult, by using mottled, ambiguously colored marbles such as cat's eyes, the democratic Circle was fastest and most accurate. Because the experiment was carefully controlled, the reason for the Circle's superiority was clearly its democratic flow of information. And there was a bonus to the Circle. When the Wheel proved superior at its simple task, only the leader felt good. The non-leaders experienced no rush of satisfaction. But when the Circle beat the other configurations on its more demanding task, higher morale was reported all around.

The Internet was only a dream when that experiment was first done. But its findings are confirmed again and again in today's wired, networked world. Several years ago, I participated in a forum on leadership in the twenty-first century. Fellow speaker Meredith Belbin, an expert on teams, offered a compelling insight. He speculated that the traditional idea of the alpha male leader may be natural to us as primates. But, he argued, this century's ever-increasing interconnectedness calls for new models, notably the "sophisticated interdependent systems of social insects."[16] Information does not just circulate within today's organizations. Because of digital technology, information increasingly flows between organizations and such outside entities as their clients and suppliers. As Belbin observed: "Information is coming in from the side instead of from the top down. Such a switch in information supply is creating pressure on the top. By losing its likely monopoly on leadership, the top can survive with credibility only by empowering the most suitable individuals and teams."

Knowledge is still power. But as knowledge becomes more widely distributed, so does the power it generates. The very idea of leadership is beginning to change as power is democratized. At such influential workplaces as Google, leadership rotates within small groups of engineers. As greater openness demystifies what leaders do, we are likely to see less time and money spent on costly, time-consuming executive searches. Leadership may come to be seen as a role that moves from one able individual in an organization to another as projects come and go. Soon the CEO may have to share responsibilities, at least for a time, with John Patrick's Sally, the one who knows everything. And should leadership become a transitory role, one likely and welcome result will be a drop in stratospheric executive compensation, one of the most corrosive facets of corporate life today.

Collegial collaboration enhances transparency, which in turn enhances success. Lack of transparency erodes trust and discourages collaboration. One place to see the transformative effect of transparency is at companies that practice so-called open-book management. As Joe Nocera explains in a 2006 column in the *New York Times*, that term, first used by a writer at *Inc.* magazine almost two decades ago, refers to the sharing of financial information with everyone in a company.[17] But effective proponents do more than throw numbers at their staff, Nocera notes. They explain what the financial information means and how employees contribute to the group's success. As evidence of the effectiveness of open-book management, Nocera reports that a 2005 survey conducted by *Inc.* found that 40 percent of the firms on its yearly list of the five hundred fastest-growing private companies employed the practice in some fashion—far more than in the business community as a whole. And it has recently been instituted at *Inc.* by Mansueto Ventures, the private firm that bought the magazine in 2006. Again and again, studies show that companies that rate high in transparency tend to outperform more opaque ones. In a global study of corporate transparency conducted in 2005, for example, the twenty-seven U.S. firms that appeared among the thirty-four most transparent companies beat the S&P 500 by 11.3 percent between February 2004 and February 2005.

More and more companies are choosing transparency for two reasons: they have less and less choice—and it works. Don Tapscott talked about its many benefits shortly after publication of his 2003 book, *The Naked Corporation: How the Age of Transparency Will Revolutionize Business.* "This isn't simply New Age stuff," he told *CIO Insight* magazine.[18] "It's about money and efficiency. When you have openness and candor, you drop transaction costs, you reduce office politics and game playing, you increase employee loyalty, you increase the effectiveness of collaboration and so on." That said, it is important to remember that, like democracy, transparency isn't easy. It requires courage and patience on the part of leaders and followers alike. It also requires a considerable investment of time, if only to share information with a larger group of people.

TRANSPARENCY'S WOES

But there is a downside to the instantaneous access to all kinds of information that is making organizations more transparent. The same forces are fast making privacy a thing of the past. Consider one mundane example. The digital technology that allows supermarkets to manage inventory as never before, stocking only the goods they currently need, also allows Big Brother to peer into the shopping cart of every patron who signs up for an electronic discount card. Thus, somewhere in the computer files of Supermarket Central is a record of how many bottles of bourbon Mrs. X purchased this week, the brand of hair dye she uses, and the fact that she recently bought a year's supply of roach poison—all information that Mrs. X might prefer to keep to herself. The grocery chain stores the specifics of every trip to the supermarket Mrs. X makes, along with records of all its other electronically linked customers, in its computer files. That information will probably remain there forever, given the indelible nature of most digital information. And there is no guarantee that the stored data about Mrs. X's shopping habits will not be hacked or misused. Look at the millions of customers of the discount shoe chain DSW whose social security numbers and other credit-card data now float through cyberspace, accessible to anyone with the computer skills of a bright fifth grader. As more and more of our personal records go online, our ability to keep our information confidential will continue to diminish, no matter how conscientiously privacy advocates strive to protect it. At the same time, the ubiquity of cell phone cameras makes each of us the potential target of amateur paparazzi, as anyone knows who's turned up on the Bad Drivers Web site.

The lack of privacy that results from transparency can be annoying, embarrassing, and infuriating. It can also be dangerous. Public access to electronic court records has given rise to such controversial Web sites as Whosearat.com. Here the public can find the names and other information about individuals who have agreed to testify against others, usually as part of plea agreements. According to the *New York Times,* the Justice Department is scrambling to get this information removed from public view, although most experts agree its publication is protected by the First Amendment.[19] The concern is that the individuals named on the site for giving evidence against accomplices and others may be subjected to "witness intimidation, retaliation and harassment." Transparency would not be a problem in a world in which everyone is decent and fair-minded. In the real world, thugs and predators have computers, too.

If the new transparency changes our expectations of privacy in ways that can be problematical, the digital technology that drives it also has an invaluable upside. One of its remarkable strengths is its ability to tap into the wisdom of crowds, in writer James Surowiecki's resonant phrase. We can access collective intelligence as never before, making primitive forms of tapping opinion, such as focus groups, obsolete. We can also benefit from the wisdom of the group in such modest but valuable forms as the aggregate restaurant ratings in the popular

Zagat guides and the collective recommendations that send many consumers to angieslist.com to find roofers and other service providers. Typically, we ease into relationships with electronic advisers. We take a chance on one of their referrals, and if we like the meal or the paint job, we feel confident using the resource again. Trust is important when you don't really know the people whose collective counsel you are taking. The blogger is a powerful but problematic presence in this vast electronic neighborhood. The blogosphere is filled with millions of voices—some brilliant, some boorish, some bigoted, some crazy. We sift through them and choose the ones that make sense to us. Those bloggers who attract large numbers of regular readers acquire enormous clout, reflected in the willingness of advertisers to buy space on their blogs.

The popular blogger has the power of an ancient Roman to turn a digital thumb up or down and determine the fate of a business or product, all at the speed of light. Commerce has already been altered by this force. Manhattan restaurant owner Paul Grieco recently told the *New York Times* how bloggers have upped the pressure on him to please those he greets at his eatery Insieme.[20] "It used to be that if something went wrong, you might lose a circle of family or friends," Grieco said. "Now, half our reservations come from the Internet, and a negative experience on a blog can affect thousands of potential customers."

The problem here, of course, is that what looks like transparency may not be. The blogger who slams a restaurant may not be a run-of-the-mill diner. He may be the unscrupulous owner of a rival restaurant who decides to whack the competition electronically, a despicable sock puppet. The digital realm is wild and minimally policed, an electronic Deadwood where things are not always what they appear to be. Any number of commentators on the difficulty of establishing identity online cite a *New Yorker* cartoon that has been taped on thousands of computers: "On the Internet nobody knows you're a dog." Genuine transparency is impossible as long as we cannot be sure that those online are who they say they are.

Although digital technology may not be the sole cause of the problem, the United States is in the throes of an expertise crisis. Because the Internet is open to everyone, it tends to be a great leveler. But when all voices have the same force, it is harder and harder to identify those who have the training, experience, and wisdom that make them truly worth listening to. Television today is full of self-appointed experts who make assured pronouncements on current events and other matters and yet have no credentials beyond a good haircut and an even better agent. The mainstream media have accelerated this devaluing of authentic expertise by treating ordinary viewers and readers as the equals of those with genuine insight and experience. Thus, CNN devotes some time that could be spent hearing expert analysis to asking viewers what they think about American immigration policy and other issues of the day. Such public involvement may massage viewers' egos and increase loyalty to the station, but, arguably, it does little to advance the audience's understanding of important, often complex issues.

This devaluing of expertise is of great concern to everyone who fears that the blogosphere may be the fatal blow to the world's great and beleaguered newspapers. Information in reputable papers is vetted by experienced journalists striving for the truth and committed to fairness. Bloggers may be committed to nothing more than making themselves heard. Former Gawker blogger and mainstream journalist Choire Sicha articulated his fears in 2006, in a far-ranging critique of blogging by Trevor Butterworth in London's *Financial Times*.[21] Blogs are a substitute for professional journalism only if you are willing to forgo much of what we receive from good newspapers today, Sicha argued. "Where is the reporting?" he asked. "Where is the reliability? The blogosphere crowd are apparently ready to live in a world without war reporting, without investigative reporting, without nearly any of the things we depend on newspapers for. The world of blogs is like an entire newspaper composed of op-eds and letters and wire service feeds." Many of us feel that blogs will be an adequate substitute for great newspapers only when they go beyond repackaging content to generate comprehensive content of their own and when they commit to high standards of accuracy, fairness, and conduct.

TRUTH AND TRANSPARENCY

On the Internet the ideas of truth and authenticity do not mean the same thing to everyone. It is a cliché of e-marketing that the public will excuse anything but hypocrisy. Candor is all, we are repeatedly told. But since who you are online is not always clear, transparency and truth may be relative. In the fall of

2007, one of the biggest stories in the business press was a possible bid by Microsoft to buy a stake in the wildly popular social-networking site Facebook. In the *Wall Street Journal,* the story was cast as a "battle of the titans between Microsoft Corp. and Google Inc." Microsoft ultimately won the right to invest $240 million in Facebook Inc., a phenomenon even by the hyperbolic standards of the Web. Founded by twenty-three-year-old Mark Zuckerberg in his Harvard dormitory room in 2004, the company has been valued at as much as $15 billion. Once open only to the invited, Facebook is now accessible to everyone. It already has 40 million users and is adding a remarkable 200,000 new participants a day.

What differentiates Facebook from other social networking sites such as MySpace, besides a residual air of exclusivity, is its transparency. On Facebook, you have to use your real name. As a result, David Kirkpatrick wrote recently in *Fortune,* "a culture of authentic identity became part of Facebook's DNA."[22] Interactions on Facebook are organized around circles of friends who keep each other informed about whom and what they are seeing, the books by their bedside, their favorite presidential candidate, and the like. Much of Facebook's magic is based on the assumption that you can trust friends and your friends' friends in ways that you can not trust the rest of the universe, wired or not.

Kirkpatrick foresees a future for Facebook in which transparency reaches new heights as new applications facilitate easier communication. This hyper-transparency could be bad for some, he predicts, especially marketers whose products are slammed by users. But it is likely that the growing millions who frequent Facebook will set their own limits on how freely on-site information is shared. Late in 2007, some 50,000 Facebook users protested the site's decision to notify their circles of friends about their online purchases. The protestors let Zuckerberg know they felt their Internet use was their own business—a vote for privacy over involuntary transparency. The company finally agreed to get permission before revealing users' purchases.

While Kirkpatrick and other card-carrying adults see Facebook as an island of authenticity in a sea of Internet uncertainty, some early adopters say "Not so fast." In a hilarious op-ed piece in the *New York Times,* recent Dartmouth graduate Alice Mathias notes that "in no time at all, the Web site has convinced its rapidly assembling adult population that it is a forum for genuine personal and professional connections."[23] Not for her cohort, it isn't. Instead, Mathias writes, "It's all comedy: making one another laugh matters more than providing useful updates about ourselves, which is why entirely phony profiles were all the rage before the grown-ups signed in. One friend announced her status as In a Relationship with Chinese Food, whose profile picture was a carry-out box." Users her age turn to Facebook for escapism, she writes: "I've always thought of [it] as on-line community theater."

Even as the value of Facebook is pushed into the stratosphere by its perceived authenticity, genuine or not, a very different notion of what is real coexists online. That is the world of Second Life, a platform or game or obsession in which people gleefully create inauthentic versions of themselves, called avatars, and spend hours at their keyboards selling virtual real estate and setting up digital shops that sell real products and even having virtual affairs with the avatars of real people other than their spouses. This would seem to give the lie to the notion that authenticity is what people want on the Internet. My sense of this brave new world (that has such avatars in it!) is that there are those who want reality and those who want role-playing and fantasy. Some people undoubtedly want both. There is a real generational difference at work here, I believe. People of my generation who suddenly have the urge to play online in the persona of an intergalactic princess reach for the telephone to call their therapists. A mostly younger generation wonders where to buy their avatar a virtual ball gown and tiara. It isn't clear to me whether spending long periods of time in Second Life will eventually change participants' ideas of what is true and what is not. We will have to see. But Second Life is a reminder that the Internet is many things to many people, and that authenticity is not the goal of everyone who goes online (ask Ms. Mathias). Niche marketing is all.

One thing I am certain of. The new technology-driven transparency will only accelerate. It has already changed our lives in countless ways and will continue to reshape us. The ubiquity of cell phones has turned public life in every major city into an odd, alienating experience in which people walk around, phone to ear, utterly engaged in a relationship with someone other than you. The new technology has also democratized power in a way that must come as a dreadful shock to those who previously monopolized it in the traditional manner. Editor and writer Harold Evans was on the mark when he observed in the *Wall Street Journal*'s 2007 Blogiversary feature that all bloggers have "a megaphone to the world."[24] However eccentric, shallow, even banal the blogger's message is, it has the ability to shape public opinion and thus to have a significant impact on the world—a far cry from the fleeting impact ordinary individuals could expect when the only outlet for their opinion was a letter to the editor of a major newspaper. And because bloggers have power, organizations are forced to react to them, whether they want to or not. Not to respond is to abdicate control of your reputation and that of your organization to someone who is far less likely to serve you well.

The lack of privacy is perhaps the most unsettling aspect of the new transparency, as we are reminded daily. We have no real expectation of privacy except when we are alone in a locked, windowless room. As Thomas L. Friedman writes in "The Whole World Is Watching," his *New York Times* column of June 27, 2007: "We're all public figures now." As a result, anyone has the ability to embarrass us, should they tilt their cell phone camera in our direction and catch us squabbling with a sales clerk or being rude to a spouse. Every day has the potential to turn into a real-life episode of *Candid Camera*, the classic, cringe-inducing television show from the 1950s on which hapless individuals were filmed without their knowledge, then had their awkward behavior broadcast for all the viewing public to see. This is a downside of transparency most of us never in our worst nightmares expected to face. It is the sort of glasshouse exposure that Brad Pitt and other celebrities have had to cope with for years, although they are at least paid handsomely for the discomfort of being public figures.

The new electronic transparency has other characteristics that both organizations and individuals are just now coming to terms with. Negative information can be spread much more rapidly than in the past, and, once it is committed to the Internet, it is there forever. Performances such as Michael Richards's racist rant in a Los Angeles comedy club will run on YouTube and its successors in perpetuity. You can hire someone to spin what comes up when you Google your name or that of your organization, but you can't really make it go away. Damaging information will be in the ether longer than a plastic bag in a landfill. You can't do anything about what others say about you, but you can at least be careful about not harming your own reputation. Indeed, we have already had to add the warning "Remember that the Internet is forever, so don't put anything on MySpace that will come back to haunt you" to the long list of things we teach our children, along with "Don't talk with your mouth full" and "Don't run with scissors."

There is another major problem with the new transparency besides its tendency to catch and preserve experience like some vast digital La Brea tar pit. That is the troubling fact that what is exposed usually seems true. Harold Evans was again on the money when he said that the information on blogs, true or false, is marked by the "spurious authenticity of electronic delivery." In a world in which organizational and personal secrets are revealed round the clock at blog speed, we have a greater responsibility than ever to vet and verify what we see.

Lies, urban legends, and distortions are as much a part of the mix as authentic revelations. Moreover, it is often impossible to determine the actual source of a nugget of information on the Web; we recently learned, for example, that companies often add to their Wikipedia entries or delete information from them without leaving tell-tale fingerprints. On the Internet propaganda often masquerades as fact. A classic example: that all Jews were warned away from the World Trade Center on 9/11, a cruel racist fabrication that appeared on many Islamist Web sites. The Internet is a dispassionate delivery system; it doesn't care whether it trades in enlightenment or lies.

As a result, governments, other institutions, and individuals must find ways to authenticate online information, much as they earlier had to devise methods to determine the authenticity of signatures and $100 bills. South Korea had to grapple with these issues in 2007 after electronic tipsters exposed prominent citizens who had claimed academic credentials they had not earned, egregious behavior in a country that worships degrees from prestigious universities. Among the cheats: a noted art historian, a famous chef, and even a celebrated Buddhist monk.[25] A South Korean prosecutor involved in the effort to prevent such fraud in the future told the *New York Times* in September 2007: "Before we struggled more with fake luxury goods. Now that we have entered the knowledge-based society, we have to deal with an overflow of fake knowledge."

The new transparency is no doubt changing us in unanticipated ways we don't yet recognize. With its millions of intrusive cameras, its constant potential for trumpeting past indiscretions through cyberspace, and its other discontents, the new reality will force us to adapt or go mad. Eventually, a new etiquette will evolve that will allow us to live more comfortably with the round-the-clock possibility of surveillance by anyone who happens to pass by. Some new method will emerge that quiets the cacophony of ever-present cell phones and lessens the pain of being "flamed" online by any malcontent who decides to go after us. Until then, we will have to be more wary, and we'll have to develop thicker skins. And since the cameras aren't going away anytime soon, we'll have to find a way to lower the blinds in our glass houses, if only in our minds.

NOTES

CREATING A CULTURE OF CANDOR

1. Shai Oster, "Chinese Protesters Harness Web as Tool," *Wall Street Journal*, June 2, 2007.
2. John Schwartz, "Transparency, Lost in the Fog," *New York Times*, April 8, 2007.
3. Barry Meier, "Internal Turmoil at Device Maker as Inquiry Grew," *New York Times*, February 28, 2006.
4. Graeme Wood, "Classify This," *Atlantic*, September 2007.
5. Mark Mazzetti, "C.I.A. Chief Tries Preaching a Culture of More Openness," *New York Times*, June 23, 2007.
6. Sarah Kershaw, "In Bid for Transparency, New York City Puts Data on Hospital Errors Online," *New York Times*, September 2, 2007.
7. Tom Lowry, "The CEO Mayor," *Business Week*, June 25, 2007.
8. Scott Shane, "Bipartisan Support Emerges for Federal Whistle-Blowers," *New York Times*, February 17, 2006.
9. Xiao Qiang, "Breaking the 'Great Firewall,'" in Tunku Varadarajan's "Happy Blogiversary," *Wall Street Journal*, July 14–15, 2007.
10. Rachel L. Swarns, "Mozambique Pays for Capitalism in Dollars and in Blood," *New York Times*, December 22, 2001.
11. Clive Thompson, "The See-Through CEO," *Fast Company*, March 2007.
12. *Mother Jones*, June 2007, cited in "A Tip for Whistleblowers: Don't," *Wall Street Journal*, May 31, 2007.
13. Anand Giridharadas, "In India, Protecting a Whistle-Blower," *New York Times*, July 5, 2007.

14. David Kirkpatrick and Daniel Roth, "Why There's No Escaping the Blog," *Fortune,* January 10, 2005.

15. Kirkpatrick and Roth, "Why There's No Escaping the Blog."

16. Vito Pilieci, "Officials Grapple With Ever-Evolving Internet," *Ottawa Citizen,* October 4, 2007.

17. Clifford Krauss, "A Blog Written From Minneapolis Rattles Canadian Liberal Party," *New York Times,* April 7, 2005.

18. Charles Fishman, "The Anarchist's Cookbook," *Fast Company,* July 2004.

19. Brad Reagan, "The Dirt on the Neighbors," *SmartMoney,* October 2007.

20. David Kesmodel and John R. Wilke, "Whole Foods Is Hot, Wild Oats a Dud—So Said 'Rahodeb,'" *Wall Street Journal,* July 12, 2007.

21. Douglas Jehl, "The Reach of War: Intelligence; Despite a Pledge to Speed Work, Fixing an Internal Problem Takes Time at the C.I.A.," *New York Times,* June 10, 2004.

22. Geraldine Fabrikant, "A 'Yes, Lord Black' Board Says 'No,'" *New York Times,* February 16, 2004.

23. Louis Lavelle, "Lessons of the 'Hollinger Chronicles,'" *Business Week,* September 13, 2004.

24. Matthew Boyle, "Growing Against the Grain," *Fortune,* May 3, 2004.

25. David Hackett Fischer, *Washington's Crossing* (Oxford, England: Oxford University Press, 2004).

26. Jennifer Reingold, "Soldiering On," *Fast Company,* September 2004.

27. G. Roth and A. Kleiner, *Car Launch: The Human Side of Managing Change* (Oxford, England: Oxford University Press, 1999), cited in Leslie Perlow and Nelson Repenning's Harvard Business School working paper "The Dynamics of Silencing Conflict," 2003.

28. Darren Dahl, "Learning to Love Whistleblowers," *Inc.,* March 2006.

29. For more about "vital lies" and how they affect families and organizational life, see Daniel Goleman's *Vital Lies, Simple Truths: The Psychology of Self-Deception* (London: Bloomsbury, 1997).

30. Claudia H. Deutsch, "At Lunch With: Leslie A. Perlow; Corporate Silence Has a Vocal Opponent," *New York Times,* August 3, 2003.

31. Deborah Solomon, Ann Carrns, and Chad Terhune, "SEC Alleges HealthSouth Faked $1.4 Billion in Profits," *Wall Street Journal,* March 20, 2003.

32. Irving Janis, *Victims of Groupthink* (Boston: Houghton Mifflin, 1983; originally published 1972).

33. Goleman, *Vital Lies, Simple Truths*. Both the Bay of Pigs fiasco and the Cuban Missile crisis are treated definitively in Robert Dallek, *An Unfinished Life: John F. Kennedy 1917–1963* (New York: Little, Brown, 2003).

34. "Judging Intelligence; The Senators' Views and Excerpts from the Report on Iraq Assessments," *New York Times*, June 10, 2004.

35. David Johnston, "The Reach of War: Conclusions; Powell's 'Solid' C.I.A. Tips Were Soft, Committee Says," *New York Times*, July 11, 2004.

36. Robert F. Kennedy, *Thirteen Days: A Memoir of the Cuban Missile Crisis* (New York: Norton, 1971).

37. Bennis discussed how Caesar, McNamara, and other leaders filtered information with Paul Michelman in "What Leaders Allow Themselves to Know," *Harvard Management Update*, February 1, 2004.

38. John Schwartz and Matthew L. Wald, "Loss of the Shuttle: The Overview; Report on Loss of Shuttle Focuses on NASA Blunders and Issues Somber Warning," *New York Times*, August 27, 2003.

SPEAKING TRUTH TO POWER

1. Richard Lacayo and Amanda Ripley, "Persons of the Year," *Time*, December 22, 2002.

2. It turns out Rumsfeld was a little late or perhaps misinformed. While I had been executive vice president for seminars at the Aspen Institute, I had quit that position some months before he asked members of the Institute's board to can me.

3. Examples in this and the following section are based on my personal experiences as originally related in James O'Toole, *Vanguard Management* (New York: Doubleday, 1985).

4. Kerry Kennedy Cuomo, *Speak Truth to Power* (New York: Crown, 2000).

5. Robin Marantz Henig, "Darwin's God," *New York Times Magazine*, March 4, 2007, p. 36.

6. Pointed out in Noel Tichy and Stratford Sherman, *Control Your Own Destiny or Someone Else Will* (New York: Doubleday, 1993).

7. I was head of seminar programs at the Aspen Institute at the time.

8. Quoted in James O'Toole, *Leadership A to Z* (Jossey-Bass, 1999).

9. Edward E. Lawler, *Rewarding Excellence: Pay Strategies for the New Economy* (San Francisco: Jossey-Bass, 2000).

10. Frank La Fusto and Carl Larsen, *When Teams Work Best* (Thousand Oaks, Calif.: Sage, 2001).

11. LRN Corporation, "The LRN 2007 Ethics and Compliance Risk Management Practices Report," 2007. Available online: www.lrn.com/insights/papers/334. Access date: December 22, 2007.

12. Robert R. Blake and Jane S. Mouton, "Effective Crisis Management," *New Management*, (3)1, 1985, p. 14.

13. Thom Shanker, "New Strategy Vindicates ex-Army Chief Shinseki," *New York Times*, January 12, 2007, p. A13.

14. Bob Woodward, *State of Denial: Bush at War, Part III* (New York: Simon & Schuster, 2006).

15. Ron Suskind, *The One Percent Doctrine: Deep Inside America's Pursuit of Its Enemies Since 9/11* (New York: Simon & Schuster, 2006).

16. Ron Suskind, *The Price of Loyalty: George W. Bush, the White House, and the Education of Paul O'Neil* (New York: Simon & Schuster, 2004).

17. David Brooks, "Building a Team of Rivals," *New York Times*, November 19, 2006.

18. Warren Bennis and Burt Nanus, *Leaders* (New York: HarperCollins, 1985).

19. Michael Powell, "Managing Up, Down and Sideways," *New York Times*, October 7, 2007, p. wk3.

20. Michael Beschloss, "Not the President's Men," *New York Times Book Review*, August 5, 2007, p. 10.

21. Stephen L. Carter, *Integrity* (New York: Basic Books, 1996).

22. Daniel Goleman, *Emotional Intelligence* (New York: Bantam Books, 1995), pp. ix–xiv. The discussion of Aristotle in the following three sections is adapted from James O'Toole, *Creating the Good Life* (New York: Rodale, 2005), pp. 152–57.

23. Frank Rich, "Is Condi Holding the Smoking Gun?" *New York Times*, May 6, 2007.

24. Richard A. Clarke, *Against All Enemies* (New York: Free Press, 2004).

25. Albert O. Hirschman, *Exit, Voice, and Loyalty* (Cambridge, Mass.: Harvard University Press, 1970).

26. "Maurice Papon," *The Economist*, February 24, 2007.

27. Carol Hymowitz, "Executives Who Build Truth-Telling Cultures Learn Fast What Works," *Wall Street Journal,* June 12, 2006, p. B1.

28. Halberstam quoted by Powell in "Managing Up, Down and Sideways."

29. Frank Rich, "The Timely Death of Gerald Ford," *New York Times,* January 7, 2007.

30. Leslie Wayne, "Unwritten Rule No. 1: Take Care of the Boss," *New York Times,* February 11, 2007.

31. Questionnaire is reproduced in Chapter 7 of James O'Toole, *Making America Work* (New York: Continuum, 1981).

32. See James O'Toole and Edward E. Lawler III, *The New American Workplace* (New York: Palgrave Macmillan, 2006).

33. Jack Stack and Bo Burlingham, *The Great Game of Business* (New York: Currency Doubleday, 1994).

34. Elizabeth Wyckoff, Trans., *Sophocles' "Antigone"* (Chicago: University of Chicago Press, 1954).

THE NEW TRANSPARENCY

1. James Taranto, editor of OpinionJournal.com, calls Drudge's a "proto-blog" in Tunku Varadarajan's "Happy Blogiversary," *Wall Street Journal,* July 14–15, 2007.

2. Tony Perry, "Navy to Mask Coronado's Swastika-Shaped Barracks," latimes.com, September 26, 2007, and "Swastika Shaped Building Oops," ker-plunk.blogspot.com, September 28, 2007.

3. Joel Kurtzman and Glenn Yago, *Global Edge: Using the Opacity Index to Manage the Risks of Cross-Border Business* (Boston: Harvard Business School Press, 2007), p. ix.

4. Joel Kurtzman, Glenn Yago, and Triphon Phumiwasana, "The Opacity Index 2004" (Cambridge, Mass.: MIT Sloan Management Review, October 2004). Available online: www.opacityindex.com/opacity _index.pdf. Access date: December 29, 2007.

5. Gordon Fairclough, "China Rescues 'Slave' Workers," *Wall Street Journal,* June 16–17, 2007.

6. Geoffrey Fowler and Juying Qin, "China Moves to Boost Transparency, but Much Is Kept Hidden," *Wall Street Journal,* April 25, 2007.

7. Geoffrey Fowler and Juying Qin, "China Pushes Openness," *Wall Street Journal,* March 1, 2007.

8. *Business Week* article in *Chindia: How China and India Are Revolutionizing Global Business,* edited by Pete Engardio (New York: McGraw-Hill, 2007).

9. Katrina vanden Heuvel, "Editor's Cut: Bloggers of Iran," May 30, 2005. Available online: www.thenation.com/blogs/edcut?bid= 7&pid=2947. Access date: December 28, 2007.

10. Seth Mydans, "Monks Are Silenced, and for Now, the Web Is, Too," *New York Times,* October 4, 2007.

11. Michael Cornfield quoted in Tom Zeller, "Are Bloggers Setting the Agenda? It Depends on the Scandal," *New York Times,* May 23, 2005.

12. David Kirkpatrick and Daniel Roth, "Why There's No Escaping the Blog," *Fortune,* January 10, 2005.

13. Marcia Stepanek, "Expert Voice: John Patrick on Weblogs," *CIO Insight,* November 1, 2003.

14. I described this experiment earlier in "Share the Power," *CIO Insight,* March 1, 2004.

15. The late Harold J. Leavitt, author, management expert, and friend, wrote an influential dissertation on the experiment.

16. Also described in "Share the Power."

17. Joe Nocera, "Want to Rally the Troops? Try Candor," *New York Times,* February 11, 2006.

18. Stepanek, "Expert Voice."

19. Adam Liptak, "Web Sites Expose Informants and Justice Dept. Raises Flag," *New York Times,* May 22, 2007.

20. Joe Drape, "Out in Front but Often Overlooked," *New York Times,* September 26, 2007.

21. Trevor Butterworth, "Blogged Off," *Financial Times,* February 18–19, 2006.

22. David Kirkpatrick, "Facebook's Plan to Hook Up the World," *Fortune,* June 11, 2007.

23. Alice Mathias, "The Fakebook Generation," *New York Times,* October 6, 2007.

24. Harold Evans, "A Spurious Megaphone," in Tunku Varadarajan's "Happy Blogiversary."

25. Su Hyun Lee, "Revelations of False Credentials Shake South Korea," *New York Times,* September 1, 2007.

THE AUTHORS

Warren Bennis is the author of *On Becoming a Leader* and *Organizing Genius* (with Pat Ward Biederman) and many other best-selling books on management and leadership. He is currently Distinguished Professor of Management at the University of Southern California and Chairman of the Board of Harvard University's Center for Public Leadership. He has consulted for many Fortune 500 companies and world leaders. He lives in Santa Monica, California.

Psychologist **Daniel Goleman** is the author of the groundbreaking and best-selling books *Emotional Intelligence* and *Social Intelligence: The New Science of Human Relationships*, among others. He is also codirector of the Consortium for Research on Emotional Intelligence in Organizations, based at Rutgers University.

James O'Toole is the Daniels Distinguished Professor of Business Ethics at the University of Denver's Daniels College of Business. He is author of seventeen books, including *Leading Change, The Executive's Compass,* and *Creating the Good Life.*

Patricia Ward Biederman, a former staff writer at the *Los Angeles Times,* is a prize-winning reporter and columnist. A longtime collaborator with Warren Bennis, she coauthored the national best-seller *Organizing Genius: The Secrets of Creative Collaboration.*